GREAT COOKING MADE EASY

PERFECT PASTA

Better Homes and Gardens
TRADEMARK

TREASURE PRESS

BETTER HOMES AND GARDENS BOOKS

Editor	Gerald M. Knox
Art Director	Ernest Shelton
Managing Editor	David A. Kirchner
Project Editors	James D. Blume, Marsha Jahns
Project Managers	Liz Anderson, Jennifer Speer Ramundt, Angela K. Renkoski

Pasta (American edition)

Editor	Barbara Atkins
Project Manager	James D. Blume
Graphic Designer	Harijs Priekulis
Electronic Text Processor	Donna Russell
Photographers	Michael Jensen, Sean Fitzgerald
Food Stylists	Marilyn Cornelius, Suzanne Finley, Janet Herwig, Maria Rolandelli

Perfect Pasta (British edition)

Project Managers	Liz Anderson, Jennifer Speer Ramundt
Assistant Art Director	Lynda Haupert
Contributing Project Editors	Irena Chalmers Books, Inc., and associates: Jean Atcheson, Irena Chalmers, Ann Chase, Mary Dauman, Cathy Garvey, Mary Goodbody, Terri Griffing, Margaret Homberg, Kathryn Knapp, Stephanie Lyness, Susan Anderson Nabel, Victoria Proctor, Elizabeth Wheeler
Electronic Text Processors	Alice Bauman, Kathy Benz, Paula Forest, Vicki Howell, Mary Mathews, Joyce Wasson

This edition first published in Great Britain in 1989 by:

Treasure Press
Michelin House
81 Fulham Road
London, SW3 6RB

Original edition published by Meredith Corporation in the United States of America.

BETTER HOMES AND GARDENS is a registered trademark in Canada, New Zealand, South Africa, and other countries.

ISBN 1 85051 438 0

Produced by Mandarin Offset
Printed and bound in Hong Kong

Pasta . . . one of the world's simplest foods! In its purest form, pasta is nothing more than a paste of flour and water.

But just because the basic formula is simple doesn't mean that pasta is limited in shape, size, or flavour. In fact, the "pastabilities" are endless.

Pasta's popularity around the world proves its versatility. Germans, Chinese, and Italians alike savour their own versions of this food.

In the pages of *Perfect Pasta,* we've captured the best of these time-tested flavour and shape combinations. You'll find recipes for such standbys as Spaghetti with Meatballs and Classic Lasagne.

We also go a step further, giving you new and creative dishes such as Taco Pasta Pie and Homemade Nut Pasta.

Perfect Pasta will help you discover and enjoy a whole world of eating far beyond the realm of plain spaghetti.

Contents

Packaged Pasta Perk-Ups

Add pizzazz to packaged pasta with these easy-on-the-cook recipes. They all start with a dried or tinned convenience product. You'll find some of these handy mixes in your local supermarket.

From there, stir in a few extra ingredients to add your personal touch. Bingo! You've got a delicious pasta dish at the double.

Chili-Spaghetti Ring

Chilli-Spaghetti Ring

The peanut topper adds crunch, flavour, and protein to this meatless main dish.

8 ounces (225g) spaghetti
2 ounces (50g) grated Edam cheese
1 ounce (25g) snipped parsley
2 tablespoons butter *or* margarine
16 ounces (450g) tinned red kidney beans, drained
8 ounces (225g) meatless spaghetti sauce
2 fluid ounces (55ml) beer *or* water
½ teaspoon chilli powder
2 ounces (50g) chopped unsalted peanuts

Cook spaghetti according to the packet directions (see photo 1). Drain in a colander (see photo 2).

Return spaghetti to pan it was cooked in. Stir in cheese, parsley, and butter or margarine (see photo 3). Press into an oiled ring mould (see photo 4). Cover and let stand about 5 minutes.

Meanwhile, for sauce, in a medium saucepan combine beans, spaghetti sauce, beer or water, and chilli powder. Bring to boiling. Reduce heat, then simmer, uncovered, about 5 minutes.

To serve, turn out spaghetti onto a platter (see photo 5). Pour sauce into centre of ring. Sprinkle with peanuts. Makes 4 main-dish servings.

1 In a large saucepan or casserole bring the amount of water the packet directs to a boil. Add the pasta and set a timer for the amount of cooking time the packet indicates. As the pasta cooks, stir it occasionally to keep it separated.

2 As soon as the pasta is done, pour the pasta and water into a colander set in a sink. Give the colander a few firm shakes to remove any remaining water, as shown. Don't rinse the pasta. Doing so would cool it and wash away important nutrients.

3 Return the drained pasta to the pan you cooked it in. Add the ingredients indicated in the recipe and stir till well combined.

4 Transfer the pasta mixture to an oiled ring mould. Using the back of a spoon, press the mixture firmly into the mould. The cheeses will help bond the pasta so it holds the shape when it's turned out.

5 To turn out the ring, place a serving dish over the top of the ring mould. Invert the ring mould and dish, then lift the ring mould away, as shown. Voilà! Enjoy beautiful moulded pasta.

Pizza Frying Pan Dinner

Turn a convenient lasagne and sauce into a terrific new dinner that looks and tastes like pizza

  6 **lasagne strips**
 16 **ounces (450g) prepared pasta sauce**
  4 **ounces (110g) chopped green pepper**
 1½ **ounces (40g) sliced stoned black olives**
  4 **ounces (110g) sliced pepperoni**
  2 **ounces (50g) tinned chopped mushrooms, drained**
  2 **ounces (50g) grated mozzarella cheese**

Break the lasagne strips crosswise into thirds. Cook according to the packet directions (see photo 1, page 8). Drain in a colander (see photo 2, page 8).

In a large frying pan stir together cooked lasagne, pasta sauce, green pepper, olives, pepperoni, and mushrooms (see photo 3, page 9). Bring to boiling. Reduce heat. Sprinkle with mozzarella cheese. Cover and cook 2 minutes more. Makes 4 main-dish servings.

Attention, Microwave Owners!

The microwave timings in this book were tested using countertop microwave ovens with 600 to 700 watts of cooking power.

The cooking times are approximate because microwave ovens vary according to manufacturer.

Herbed Salmon And Noodles

In a hurry for dinner? This creamy meal-in-a-tin takes only about 20 minutes to make.

  8 **ounces (225g) green noodles**
 14 **ounces (395g) tinned chicken in mushroom sauce**
 10 **ounces (275g) frozen mixed vegetables**
  ½ **teaspoon dried marjoram, crushed**
15½ **ounces (435g) tinned salmon, drained, flaked, and skin and bones removed**
  8 **ounces (225g) cottage cheese**
 1½ **ounces (40g) prepared fried onions**

In a large saucepan cook pasta from packet according to directions (see photo 1, page 8). Drain in a colander (see photo 2, page 8).

Return pasta to the saucepan it was cooked in. Stir in chicken in mushroom sauce, vegetables, marjoram, and ½ pint (275ml) *water* (see photo 3, page 9). Bring to boiling. Reduce heat, then simmer, uncovered, for 8 minutes, while stirring frequently. Stir in salmon and cottage cheese. Heat through. Sprinkle with fried onions. Makes 6 main-dish servings.

Microwave Directions: On the stove-top, cook noodles according to packet directions. Place noodles and chicken in mushroom sauce in a 3¼ pint (1.75l) nonmetal casserole. Stir in vegetables and marjoram. Cook, uncovered, 7 to 9 minutes more or until vegetables are nearly tender, stirring once. Stir in salmon and cottage cheese. Cook, uncovered, until heated through. Let stand, covered, 5 minutes before serving. Sprinkle with onions.

Mexicali Bake

1 pound (450g) pork sausage meat
1 medium onion, chopped
5 ounces (150g) Primula cheese spread
8 ounces (225g) spaghetti
16 ounces (450g) prepared pasta sauce
2 ounces (50g) tinned chopped
mushrooms
12 ounces (350g) tinned sweet corn with
peppers
3.9 ounces (100g) green chilli peppers,
rinsed, seeded, chopped, and fried
2 ounces (50g) coarsely crushed chilli-
flavoured crisps
Grated Parmesan cheese

In a large frying pan cook sausage and onion until sausage is brown and onion is tender. Drain off fat. Stir in cheese spread. Set aside.

Cook spaghetti according to the packet directions (see photo 1, page 8). Drain in a colander (see photo 2, page 8).

Return spaghetti to the pan it was cooked in. Stir in sausage mixture, pasta sauce, mushrooms, *undrained* corn, and green chilli peppers (see photo 3, page 9).

Spoon into a 12x7½x2-inch (30x19x5cm) baking dish. Sprinkle with grated Parmesan cheese. Bake in a 350°F (180°C) gas mark 4 oven 30 minutes or until heated through. Sprinkle with crushed crisps. Makes 6 main-dish servings.

Microwave Directions: Using a 5 pint (2.75l) nonmetal casserole, micro-cook sausage and onion, covered, on 100% power (HIGH) for 4 to 6 minutes or until no pink remains, stirring twice. Drain off fat. Stir in cheese spread. Set aside. On the stove-top cook spaghetti according to the packet directions (see photo 1, page 8). Drain in a colander (see photo 2, page 8). Stir cooked spaghetti, pasta sauce, mushrooms, *undrained* corn, and chilli peppers into the sausage mixture (see photo 3, page 9). Micro-cook, covered, on 100% power (HIGH) for 5 minutes. Stir. Sprinkle with grated Parmesan cheese. Cook, covered, until heated through. Sprinkle with chilli-flavoured crisps.

Macaroni and Chicken Salad

Surprise! This tasty salad starts with a packet of macaroni and cheese.

7 ounces (200g) macaroni
1 packet cheese sauce mix
6 fluid ounces (165ml) milk
1 ounce (25g) butter *or* margarine,
softened
10 ounces (275g) chopped cooked chicken
5 ounces (150g) sliced celery
8 ounces (225g) soured cream
3 spring onions, sliced
½ teaspoon dried dill
Lettuce leaves

Cook macaroni from packet according to directions (see photo 1, page 8). Drain in a colander (see photo 2, page 8).

Return macaroni to the pan it was cooked in. Stir in cheese sauce mix from packet, milk, and butter or margarine (see photo 3, page 9).

In a large mixing bowl combine macaroni mixture, chicken, celery, soured cream, spring onion, and dill. Toss until combined. Cover and chill several hours or overnight.

To serve, line 5 salad plates with lettuce leaves. Spoon salad mixture onto each plate. Makes 5 main-dish servings.

Cook-and-Toss Pasta

The folklore is that if you throw cooked pasta against the wall and it sticks, the pasta is done.

But in favour of properly cooked pasta (and clean walls), we say the judgement is better left to your teeth. Only they can tell when the pasta is tender but still slightly firm. And that's when it's just right to toss with the simple, but oh-so-tasty ingredients you'll find in these no-fuss recipes.

Fettuccine Alfredo

Fettuccine Alfredo

The cheese, cream, and butter thicken and form a rich sauce when tossed with the hot pasta.

5 pints (2.75l) water
1 teaspoon salt
1 tablespoon cooking oil (optional)
8 ounces (225g) packaged fettuccine *or* ¾ recipe Egg Pasta, cut into fettuccine (see pages 68 and 69)
2 ounces (50g) grated Parmesan cheese
3 fluid ounces (75ml) single cream *or* whipping cream, at room temperature
1½ ounces (40g) butter *or* margarine, cut up and at room temperature
Fresh coarsely ground black pepper

In a large saucepan bring water and salt to boil. If desired, add oil to help keep pasta separated.

Add pasta a little at a time, so water does not stop boiling (see photo 1). Reduce the heat slightly and continue boiling, uncovered, stirring occasionally, until pasta is al dente (see photo 2). Allow 8 to 10 minutes for packaged fettuccine or 1½ to 2 minutes for Egg Pasta fettuccine.

Immediately drain (see photo 2, page 8). Return pasta to the hot saucepan. Add Parmesan cheese, single cream or whipping cream, and butter or margarine. Toss gently until pasta is well coated (see photo 3). Transfer to a warm serving dish. Sprinkle with pepper. Serve immediately. Makes 4 main-dish servings.

1 When the water boils vigorously, add the pasta a little at a time, so the water does not stop boiling. Hold long pasta at one end and dip the other end into the water, as shown. As the pasta softens, gently curl it around the inside of the pan and into the water.

2 Taste pasta often near the end of the cooking time to test for taste. Pasta is done when it is tender but still slightly firm. Italians call this stage al dente (ahl DEN tay), which means "to the tooth."

Hot Tips on Pasta

Here are three simple tricks for keeping cooked pasta hot:
● Drain the pasta quickly. Don't let it stand in the colander longer than is necessary.
● Return the pasta to the hot cooking pan immediately. The heat of the pan will keep the whole recipe warm.
● Always use a warm serving dish. To warm your serving dish, simply run hot water into it. Let it stand a few minutes to absorb the heat. Then empty the dish and wipe it dry. Add your cooked pasta and serve immediately.

3 Return the pasta to the hot pan in which it was cooked. Add the remaining in-gredients, then toss gently until everything is combined and the pasta is well coated.

Grecian Noodles

You can make this with either packaged or homemade pasta. If you use homemade, check the page numbers for both the recipe and the shaping or cutting method.

5 **pints (2.75l) water**
1 **teaspoon salt**
½ **teaspoon dried oregano, crushed**
¼ **teaspoon garlic powder**
1 **tablespoon cooking oil (optional)**
4 **ounces (110g) packaged green noodles** *or* ¼ **recipe Pasta Verde, cut into noodles (see pages 76 and 69)**
2 **ounces (50g) crumbled feta cheese**
1 **medium tomato, peeled, seeded, and chopped**
1 **ounce (25g) sliced stoned black olives**
1 **tablespoon olive oil** *or* **cooking oil**
⅛ **teaspoon pepper**

In a large saucepan bring water, salt, oregano, and garlic powder to the boil. If desired, add 1 tablespoon cooking oil to help keep the pasta separated.

Add pasta a little at a time, so water does not stop boiling (see photo 1, page 14). Reduce the heat slightly and continue boiling, uncovered, stirring occasionally, until pasta is al dente (see photo 2, page 14). Allow 6 to 8 minutes for packaged noodles or 1½ to 2 minutes for Pasta Verde noodles.

Immediately drain (see photo 2, page 8). Return pasta to the hot saucepan. Add cheese, tomato, olives, 1 tablespoon olive oil or cooking oil, and pepper. Toss gently until combined (see photo 3, page 15). Transfer to a warm serving dish. Serve immediately. Makes 4 side-dish servings.

Herb-Buttered Pasta

5 **pints (2.75l) water**
1 **teaspoon salt**
1 **tablespoon cooking oil (optional)**
4 **ounces (110g) packaged vermicelli** *or* ¼ **recipe Tomato-Herb Pasta, cut into linguine (see pages 79 and 69)**
1½ **ounces (40g) butter** *or* **margarine, cut up and at room temperature**
2 **tablespoons grated Parmesan cheese**
¼ **teaspoon dried rosemary, crushed**
¼ **teaspoon dried thyme, crushed**

In a large saucepan bring water and salt to the boil. If desired, add cooking oil to help keep the pasta separated.

Add pasta a little at a time, so water does not stop boiling (see photo 1, page 14). Reduce the heat slightly and continue boiling, uncovered, stirring occasionally, until pasta is al dente (see photo 2, page 14). Allow 5 to 7 minutes for packaged vermicelli or 1½ to 2 minutes for Tomato-Herb linguine.

Immediately drain (see photo 2, page 8). Return pasta to the hot saucepan. Add cut-up butter, cheese, rosemary, and thyme. Toss gently until pasta is well coated (see photo 3, page 15). Transfer to a warm serving dish. Serve immediately. Makes 4 side-dish servings.

Everyday Spaghetti with Meat Sauce

For an easy side dish, leave out the sausage and use only 4 ounces (110g) of pasta.

5 pints (2.75l) water
1 teaspoon salt
1 tablespoon cooking oil (optional)
6 ounces (175g) packaged spaghetti *or* penne
¾ pint (425ml) meatless spaghetti sauce
¾ pound (350g) sausages, cooked and cut into 1-inch (2.5cm) pieces
4 ounces (110g) tinned sliced mushrooms, drained
1 ounce (25g) grated Parmesan cheese

In a large saucepan bring water and salt to the boil. If desired, add cooking oil to help keep the pasta separated.

Add pasta a little at a time, so water does not stop boiling (see photo 1, page 14). Reduce the heat slightly and continue boiling, uncovered, stirring occasionally, until pasta is al dente (see photo 2, page 14). Allow 10 to 12 minutes for spaghetti or 14 minutes for penne.

Meanwhile, in a medium saucepan combine spaghetti sauce, sausage pieces, and drained mushrooms; heat through.

Immediately drain pasta (see photo 2, page 8). Return pasta to the hot saucepan.

Spoon sauce over cooked pasta. Toss gently until pasta is well coated (see photo 3, page 15). Transfer to a warm serving dish. Sprinkle with cheese. Makes 4 main-dish servings.

Fusilli with Poppy Seed And Almonds

A rich-tasting, mild-flavoured pasta dish that's great with a joint of lamb.

5 pints (2.75l) water
1 teaspoon salt
1 tablespoon cooking oil (optional)
4 ounces (110g) packaged fusilli *or* spaghetti
1½ ounces (40g) cream cheese with chives, softened
3 tablespoons milk
1 ounce (25g) sliced almonds, toasted
½ teaspoon poppy seed

In a large saucepan bring water and salt to the boil. If desired, add cooking oil to help keep the pasta separated.

Add pasta a little at a time, so water does not stop boiling (see photo 1, page 14). Reduce the heat slightly and continue boiling, uncovered, stirring occasionally, until pasta is al dente (see photo 2, page 14). Allow 15 minutes for fusilli or 10 to 12 minutes for spaghetti.

Immediately drain (see photo 2, page 8). Return pasta to the hot saucepan.

Stir together cream cheese and milk. Add cream cheese mixture, almonds, and poppy seed to hot pasta. Toss gently until pasta is well coated (see photo 3, page 15). Transfer to a warm serving dish. Serve immediately. Makes 4 side-dish servings.

Pasta Salads

Today's pasta salads go far beyond good old macaroni salad. And this selection is no different.

Our recipe parade displays colourful combinations of cool pasta, fresh fruits or vegetables, and mouth-watering dressings.

In fact, you might want to keep one of these pasta salads stashed away in the refrigerator. When you have a midnight craving for pasta, you can satisfy your appetite in a jiffy.

*Greek-Style
Rigatoni Salad*

Greek-Style Rigatoni Salad

3	ounces (75g) rigatoni *or* ziti
3	ounces (75g) torn Webb lettuce *or* fresh spinach
2	small tomatoes, peeled, seeded, and chopped
1½	ounces (40g) sliced stoned black olives
2	ounces (50g) crumbled feta cheese
3	tablespoons olive oil *or* salad oil
3	tablespoons white wine vinegar
½	teaspoon dried oregano, crushed
¼	teaspoon onion powder
⅛	teaspoon pepper

If using ziti, break into 1½-inch (4cm) pieces. Cook pasta in boiling salted water until al dente (*see* photos 1–2, page 14). Allow 15 minutes for rigatoni or 14 minutes for ziti. Immediately drain. Rinse with cold water, then drain well (*see* photo 1).

In a medium mixing bowl combine cooked pasta, lettuce or spinach, tomatoes, olives, and feta cheese.

For dressing, in a screw-top jar combine olive oil or salad oil, vinegar, oregano, onion powder, and pepper. Cover. Shake to mix (*see* photo 2).

Pour dressing over pasta mixture, then toss gently until all ingredients are well coated (*see* photo 3). Cover and chill several hours (*see* photo 4). Stir occasionally and just before serving. Makes 4 side-dish servings.

1 After draining the hot cooked pasta in a colander, rinse it with cold water. Then drain it well by giving the colander a few shakes. Rinsing quickly cools the hot pasta and helps keep it from sticking together in the salad.

2 To shake together a salad dressing, place all the dressing ingredients in a small screw-top jar. Cover the jar and shake to mix the ingredients well.

3 Pour the salad dressing over the pasta mixture, as shown. Then toss gently until all the ingredients are coated with the dressing.

4 Cover the salad bowl tightly with clingfilm or a tight-fitting lid. Chill the salad thoroughly. Use a wooden, glass, plastic, or ceramic bowl for storing the salad. Some metal containers rust when exposed to the acid in vinegar.

Creamy Macaroni Salad

3 ounces (75g) macaroni *or* conchigliette
3 ounces (75g) diced cheddar cheese
2 ounces (50g) chopped celery
2 tablespoons sliced spring onion
4 ounces (110g) mayonnaise
2 fluid ounces (55ml) salad cream
½ teaspoon prepared mustard
Several dashes bottled hot pepper sauce

Cook pasta in boiling salted water until al dente (see photos 1–2, page 14). Allow 10 minutes for macaroni or 8 to 9 minutes for conchigliette. Immediately drain. Rinse with cold water, then drain well (see photo 1, page 20).

In a large mixing bowl combine cooked pasta, cheese, celery, and spring onion.

For dressing, in a small bowl combine mayonnaise, creamy salad dressing, mustard, and hot pepper sauce.

Pour dressing over pasta mixture, then toss gently until all ingredients are well coated (see photo 3, page 21). Cover and chill several hours or overnight (see photo 4, page 21). Stir just before serving. Makes 4 side-dish servings.

Fruit and Pasta Toss

You get more flavour in every bite because the shell-shaped pasta traps the sweet and spicy dressing.

2 ounces (50g) packaged conchiglie
8 ounces (225g) tinned pineapple chunks in juice
1 medium orange, peeled and sectioned
3 ounces (75g) seedless grapes, halved
2 tablespoons honey
¼ teaspoon ground allspice
2 ounces (50g) broken walnuts

Cook pasta in boiling salted water until al dente (see photos 1–2, page 14). Allow 12 to 14 minutes. Immediately drain. Rinse with cold water, then drain well (see photo 1, page 20).

Drain pineapple, reserving *2 tablespoons* juice. In a large mixing bowl combine cooked pasta, pineapple, orange, and grapes.

For dressing, in a screw-top jar combine reserved juice, honey, and allspice. Cover and shake to mix well (see photo 2, page 20). Pour dressing over pasta mixture, then toss gently until all ingredients are well coated (see photo 3, page 21). Cover and chill several hours or overnight (see photo 4, page 21). Stir in walnuts just before serving. Makes 4 side-dish servings.

Don't Blame the Pasta

You might picture pasta as a culprit waiting to wrap its calories around your hips, thighs, and waist.

But pasta doesn't deserve that reputation. Three ounces (75g) of cooked noodles contains a mere 100 calories.

Pasta also contributes carbohydrates, protein, and vitamins to your diet, besides.

Of course, do watch out for the calorie-laden toppings and rich sauces that often smother pasta. They can prove to be the real calorie culprits.

Italian Rotelle Salad

A favourite salad to make at home.

3   ounces (75g) packaged rotelle *or* ¼ recipe Herb Pasta, cut into farfalle (see pages 71 and 77)
9   ounces (250g) artichoke hearts
12 cherry tomatoes, halved
4   ounces (110g) provolone cheese, cut into strips, *or* cheddar cheese, cut into ½-inch (1cm) cubes
1½ ounces (40g) sliced stoned black olives
4   ounces (110g) tinned sliced mushrooms, drained
2   ounces (50g) sliced salami, cut into 2-inch (5cm) strips
8   fluid ounces (220ml) Italian salad dressing
2   hard-boiled eggs, sliced (optional)

If using rotelle, cook pasta and artichoke hearts in boiling salted water until artichokes are done and pasta is al dente (see photos 1–2, page 14). Allow 8 to 10 minutes. (*Or,* if using Herb Pasta farfalle, cook artichoke hearts in boiling salted water for 6 minutes. Add pasta and cook 2 minutes more or until artichokes are done and pasta is al dente.)

Immediately drain. Rinse with cold water, then drain well (see photo 1, page 20).

Transfer cooked pasta and artichoke hearts to a large mixing bowl. Add tomatoes, cheese, olives, mushrooms, and salami.

Pour salad dressing over pasta mixture, then toss gently until all ingredients are well coated (see photo 3, page 21). Cover and chill several hours or overnight (see photo 4, page 21). Stir occasionally and just before serving. If desired, top with egg slices. Makes 8 side-dish servings.

Chicken Ditalini Salad

Chill the tomatoes so they're cold when you're ready to make the tomato-flower serving containers.

2   ounces (50g) packaged ditalini *or* ⅛ recipe Pineapple Pasta, cut into tripolini (see pages 78 and 77)
8   ounces (225g) chopped cooked chicken
2   ounces (50g) finely chopped celery
2   tablespoons sliced spring onion
4   fluid ounces (110ml) mayonnaise *or* salad dressing
1   tablespoon milk
2   teaspoons prepared mustard
¼   teaspoon salt
⅛   teaspoon pepper
4   medium tomatoes
    Lettuce leaves

Cook pasta in boiling salted water until al dente (see photos 1–2, page 14). Allow 7 to 9 minutes for ditalini or 2 to 3 minutes for Pineapple Pasta tripolini. Immediately drain. Rinse with cold water, then drain well (see photo 1, page 20).

In a large mixing bowl combine cooked pasta, chicken, celery, and spring onion.

For dressing, in a small mixing bowl stir together mayonnaise or salad dressing, milk, mustard, salt, and pepper.

Pour dressing over pasta mixture, then toss gently until all ingredients are well coated (see photo 3, page 21). Cover and chill several hours or overnight (see photo 4, page 21).

To serve, make tomato flowers. Place tomatoes, stem end down, on a cutting surface. With a sharp knife, cut each tomato into 6 wedges, cutting to but not through the stem end of the tomato. Transfer to lettuce-lined salad plates. Spread tomato wedges apart slightly. Spoon equal portions of the pasta mixture into each tomato. Makes 4 main-dish servings.

Pasta Pies

Move over pastry crusts! Pasta is taking your place in these trouble-free main-dish pies.

Just toss cooked pasta with an egg, press it into a pie plate, and bake. As the pasta mixture cooks, it sets, forming a firm crust that's perfect for holding hearty fillings.

Spinach Pasta Pie

Spinach Pasta Pie

6 ounces (175g) packaged spaghettini *or* ½ recipe Corn Pasta, cut into linguine (see pages 70 and 69)
1 ounce (25g) butter *or* margarine
1 beaten egg
1 ounce (25g) grated Parmesan cheese
4 ounces (110g) fresh spinach *or* 5 ounces (150g) frozen chopped spinach
2 spring onions, thinly sliced
1 ounce (25g) snipped parsley
8 ounces (225g) cream cheese, softened
2 eggs
4 fluid ounces (110ml) milk *or* single cream
½ teaspoon dried oregano, crushed

Cook pasta in boiling salted water until al dente (see photos 1–2, page 14). Allow 10 to 12 minutes for spaghettini or 1½ to 2 minutes for linguine. Immediately drain. Return to the hot saucepan. Add butter or margarine, then toss until melted. Add 1 egg and Parmesan cheese, then toss until coated. Press onto the bottom and up the sides of an ungreased 10-inch (25.5cm) quiche dish or pie plate (see photo 1). Bake in a 375°F (190°C) gas mark 5 oven for 7 to 10 minutes or until set.

Meanwhile, rinse and chop fresh spinach. In a medium saucepan cook spinach, covered, with just the water that clings to the leaves about 2 minutes. Reduce heat and cook 3 to 5 minutes more or until tender, stirring frequently. (*Or*, cook frozen spinach according to packet directions.) Drain well (see photo 2). Stir in spring onion and parsley.

In a bowl beat cream cheese and 2 eggs with an electric mixer on medium speed until combined. Stir in spinach mixture, milk or cream, oregano, ½ teaspoon *salt*, and ⅛ teaspoon *pepper*. Pour into pasta shell. Cover edge with foil (see photo 3). Bake in a 375°F (190°C) gas mark 5 oven 25 to 30 minutes or until knife inserted near centre comes out clean; let stand 10 minutes (see photo 4). Makes 6 main-dish servings.

1 Transfer the cooked pasta mixture to the quiche dish or pie plate. Using a rubber spatula or wooden spoon, firmly press the mixture onto the bottom and up the sides of the dish, forming a crust. Build the edges high to hold the filling.

2 Place the cooked spinach in a colander. Using the back of a wooden spoon or a rubber spatula, press the spinach against the sides and bottom of the colander until all water is squeezed out.

Taco Pasta Pie

For a flavourful finish to this colourful pie, dollop some soured cream on top.

6	ounces (175g) packaged spaghetti *or* ½ recipe Pasta Diable, cut into linguine (see pages 70 and 69)
1	ounce (25g) butter *or* margarine
1	beaten egg
2	ounces (50g) grated cheddar cheese
¾	pound (350g) minced beef
1	chopped onion
4	ounces (110g) green chilli peppers
2	ounces (50g) chopped green pepper
8	ounces (225g) tinned sieved tomatoes
1	teaspoon chilli powder
¼	teaspoon salt
2	ounces (50g) grated cheddar cheese
1	ounce (25g) sliced stoned black olives
1	small tomato, seeded and chopped

Cook pasta in boiling salted water until al dente (see photos 1–2, page 14). Allow 10 to 12 minutes for packaged spaghetti or 1½ to 2 minutes for Pasta Diable linguine. Immediately drain. Return to hot saucepan. Add butter or margarine, then toss until melted. Add egg, then toss until coated. Press onto the bottom and up the sides of an ungreased 10-inch (25.5cm) pie plate (see photo 1). Sprinkle 2 ounces (50g) cheddar cheese over bottom of crust. Bake in a 375°F (190°C) gas mark 5 oven for 7 to 10 minutes or until set.

Meanwhile, in a 10-inch (25.5cm) frying pan cook minced beef, onion, chilli peppers, and green pepper until beef is brown and vegetables are tender. Drain off the fat. Stir in sieved tomatoes, chilli powder, and salt, then heat until warmed through.

Transfer mixture to prepared shell. Cover edge with foil (see photo 3). Bake in a 375° (190°C) gas mark 5 oven for 15 minutes. Sprinkle with 2 ounces (50g) cheddar cheese and olives. Bake 2 minutes more or till cheese melts. Sprinkle with chopped tomato. Makes 6 main-dish servings.

3 Fold a 12-inch-long (30cm) piece of foil into quarters. Cut a 4½-inch-long (11cm) wedge out of the folded corner. Unfold the foil. There will be a circle in the centre. Lay it over the pie so the foil covers the edge to prevent overbrowning.

4 To test if cooked, insert a knife near the centre of the pie, about ½ inch (1cm) deep. If the knife comes out clean, the pie is done. If the knife comes out with filling on it, bake the pie a few minutes longer. When the pie is done, let it stand for 10 minutes so that it sets up and holds a cut edge.

Start-by-Sautéing Sauces

These sumptuous pasta sauces are deceitfully simple to make, yet sinfully delicious to eat.

Create the flavour by sautéing streaky bacon, garlic, and onion over high heat. Make a rich sauce by adding ingredients such as cream, cheese, or eggs. Then toss with cooked pasta for a sensational meal—pronto.

*Rotelle Primavera
with Sausage*

With Sausage

Here's a scrumptious meal-in-a-dish—meat, vegetables, and pasta all in one.

3 **beaten eggs**
4 **fluid ounces (110ml) whipping cream**
2 **ounces (50g) grated Parmesan cheese**
⅛ **teaspoon pepper**
6 **ounces (175g) broccoli florets**
6 **ounces (175g) thinly sliced carrots**
¾ **pound (350g) spicy sausages cut into ¼-inch (½cm) slices**
2 **ounces (50g) chopped onion**
1 **clove garlic, minced**
3 **ounces (75g) sliced fresh mushrooms**
6 **ounces (175g) rotelle *or* ruote**

In a medium mixing bowl combine eggs and cream. Mix well. Stir in Parmesan cheese and pepper (see photo 1). Set aside.

In a medium saucepan cook broccoli and carrots in a small amount of boiling salted water about 5 minutes or until tender. Drain.

In a 10-inch (25.5 cm) frying pan cook sausage, onion, and garlic for 5 minutes. Add mushrooms and cook about 5 minutes more or until sausage is brown and vegetables are tender (see photo 2). Drain off fat. Add broccoli and carrots to sausage mixture in frying pan. Keep warm.

Meanwhile, cook rotelle or ruote in boiling salted water until al dente (see photos 1–2, page 14). Allow 8 to 10 minutes for rotelle or 12 minutes for ruote. Immediately drain. Return pasta to the hot saucepan. Add sausage-vegetable mixture (see photo 3). Pour egg mixture over pasta. Toss gently until well mixed (see photo 4). Serve immediately. Makes 4 main-dish servings.

1 Add the cheese and seasonings to the egg-cream mixture and mix well. When this mixture is tossed with the hot cooked pasta, it thickens and forms a sauce that clings to the pasta. Italians typically thicken sauces with this type of egg-cream mixture instead of with flour or cornflour.

2 Cook meat or vegetables or both until meat is brown and vegetables are tender, stirring occasionally. Cooking food quickly over high heat in a small amount of fat is known as sautéing.

3 Return the drained hot pasta to the pan it was cooked in. Then add the meat-vegetable or other mixture.

4 Toss the entire mixture gently until it is well mixed and the pasta is completely coated.

Four-Cheese Tagliatelle

A truly wonderful blend of cheeses.

2   **spring onions, sliced**
½   **ounce (10g) butter *or* margarine**
¼   **pint (150ml) single cream**
2   **ounces (50g) grated Gouda *or* fontina cheese**
3   **ounces (75g) crumbled Gorgonzola cheese**
3   **ounces (75g) grated mozzarella cheese**
2   **ounces (50g) grated Parmesan cheese**
8   **ounces (225g) packaged tagliatelle *or* ½ recipe Whole Grain Pasta, cut into tagliatelle (see pages 71 and 69)**

In a 10-inch (25.5cm) frying pan cook spring onion in hot butter or margarine until tender (see photo 2, page 30). Reduce heat to low. Stir in cream. Add Gouda or fontina cheese, Gorgonzola cheese, mozzarella cheese, and Parmesan cheese. Cook and stir until cheeses melt. Remove from heat. Set aside.

Meanwhile, cook pasta in boiling salted water until al dente (see photos 1–2, page 14). Allow 6 to 8 minutes for packaged tagliatelle or 1½ to 2½ minutes for Whole Grain Pasta tagliatelle. Immediately drain. Return pasta to the hot saucepan. Add cheese mixture (see photo 3, page 31). Toss gently until well mixed (see photo 4, page 31). Serve immediately. Makes 4 main-dish servings or 8 side-dish servings.

Microwave Directions: (See tip, page 10.) In a 2½-pint (1.4l) nonmetal casserole combine onion and butter. Micro-cook, uncovered, on 100% power (HIGH) for 1½ to 2 minutes or until tender. Stir in *4 fluid ounces (110 ml)* cream, then the Gouda or fontina cheese, Gorgonzola cheese, mozzarella cheese, and Parmesan cheese. Cook, uncovered, for 2 to 2½ minutes more or until cheeses melt, stirring 3 times. Meanwhile, on the *stove-top,* cook pasta as above. Immediately drain. Return to the hot saucepan. Add cheese mixture (see photo 3, page 31). Toss gently until well mixed (see photo 4, page 31). Serve immediately.

Linguine with Clam Sauce

¾   **pint (425ml) shucked clams *or* 15 ounces (375g) tinned clams in brine, finely chopped**
2   **ounces (50g) chopped onion**
2   **cloves garlic, minced**
½   **teaspoon dried basil *or* oregano, crushed**
⅛   **teaspoon ground red pepper**
2   **tablespoons olive oil *or* cooking oil**
3   **fluid ounces (75ml) dry white wine**
2   **tablespoons snipped parsley**
8   **ounces (225g) packaged linguine *or* ⅓ recipe Lemon Pasta, cut into linguine (see pages 78 and 69)**

Drain shucked or canned clams, reserving 4 fluid ounces (110ml) clam liquid. Cut up whole clams. Set aside.

In a 10-inch (25.5cm) frying pan cook onion, garlic, basil or oregano, and red pepper in hot olive oil or cooking oil about 5 minutes or until tender (see photo 2, page 30). Carefully add reserved clam liquid, wine, and parsley. Bring to boiling and boil 4 minutes. Reduce heat, then add clams. Simmer, stirring occasionally, about 2 minutes.

Meanwhile, cook pasta in boiling salted water until al dente (see photos 1–2, page 14). Allow 8 to 10 minutes for packaged linguine or 1½ to 2 minutes for Lemon Pasta linguine. Immediately drain. Return pasta to hot saucepan. Add clam mixture (see photo 3, page 31). Toss gently until well mixed (see photo 4, page 31). Serve immediately. Makes 3 main-dish servings.

Oriental-Style Vegetables and Pasta

3   ounces (75g) packaged spaghetti *or* spaghettini, broken into 3-inch (7.5cm) lengths
3   ounces (75g) sliced fresh mushrooms
4   ounces (110g) chopped green pepper
½   ounce (10g) butter *or* margarine
3   ounces (75g) fresh *or* frozen mange tout cut crosswise into thirds
1   tablespoon soy sauce
1   teaspoon red wine vinegar
¼   teaspoon mustard powder
⅛   teaspoon ground ginger

Cook pasta in boiling salted water until al dente (see photos 1–2, page 14). Allow 10 to 12 minutes for packaged spaghetti or 8 to 10 minutes for packaged spaghettini.

Meanwhile, in a 10-inch (25.5cm) frying pan cook mushrooms and green pepper in hot butter or margarine over medium-high heat about 3 minutes or until tender, stirring frequently (see photo 2, page 30). Add mange tout. Cook and stir for 1 to 2 minutes more. Stir in soy sauce, vinegar, mustard powder, and ginger. Remove pan from heat.

Immediately drain pasta. Return pasta to the hot saucepan. Add mushroom mixture (see photo 3, page 31). Toss gently until well mixed (see photo 4, page 31). Serve immediately. Makes 4 side-dish servings.

Microwave Directions: (See tip, page 10.) On the *stove-top,* cook pasta as above. Meanwhile, in a 3¼-pint (1.75l) nonmetal casserole combine mushrooms, green pepper, and butter or margarine. Micro-cook, covered, on 100% power (HIGH) for 2 to 3 minutes or until tender, stirring once. Add mange tout. Cook, covered, 2 minutes more, stirring once. Stir in soy sauce, vinegar, mustard powder, and ginger. Immediately drain pasta. Return pasta to the hot saucepan. Add mushroom mixture (see photo 3, page 31). Toss gently until well mixed (photo 4, page 31). Serve immediately.

Carbonara-Style Penne

Savour the rich, full flavour of carbonara—a pasta dish with white cheese sauce and bits of bacon or ham.

4   beaten eggs
2   fluid ounces (55ml) whipping cream
3   ounces (75g) grated Parmesan cheese
6   rashers streaky bacon, cut crosswise into thin strips
8   ounces (225g) packaged penne *or* ½ recipe Garlic Pasta, cut into fettuccine (see pages 72 and 69)
Freshly ground black pepper
Snipped parsley

In a medium mixing bowl combine eggs and cream. Mix well. Stir in Parmesan cheese (see photo 1, page 30). Set aside.

In a 10-inch (25.5cm) frying pan cook bacon about 3 minutes or until brown and crisp (see photo 2, page 30). Remove from pan and drain on kitchen paper.

Meanwhile, cook pasta in boiling salted water until al dente (see photos 1–2, page 14). Allow 14 minutes for penne or 1½ to 2 minutes for Garlic Pasta fettuccine. Immediately drain. Return pasta to the hot saucepan. Add bacon (see photo 3, page 31). Pour egg mixture over pasta all at once. Toss gently until well mixed (see photo 4, page 31). Sprinkle with pepper. Garnish with snipped parsley. Serve immediately. Makes 4 main-dish servings.

Simmered Sauces

All good cooks know that there are some things you just can't rush. A good tomato sauce, for instance, needs time to simmer so its flavours blend to perfection.

That's the formula we followed to create these tasty simmered sauces. You'll find all your favourite tomato sauces and more. There's even a rich yet mellow-flavoured whisky and cream sauce.

Although these sauces take some time to make, we're sure you'll agree the flavour is well worth the wait. And to prepare yourself for the times when you can't wait, make the tomato-based sauces ahead, then chill or freeze.

*Old-Fashioned
Spaghetti with Meatballs*

Old-Fashioned Spaghetti With Meatballs

     3   **ounces (75g) fresh mushrooms**
     1   **small green pepper**
     1   **small onion**
     1   **clove garlic, minced**
     2   **tablespoons butter *or* margarine**
    16   **ounces (450g) tinned tomatoes, cut up**
    15   **ounces (425g) tinned sieved tomatoes**
     1   **teaspoon caster sugar**
     1   **teaspoon dried basil, crushed**
    ½   **teaspoon dried marjoram, crushed**
    ½   **teaspoon dried oregano, crushed**
     1   **beaten egg**
     1   **ounce (25g) soft breadcrumbs**
     2   **tablespoons snipped parsley**
    ¼   **teaspoon ground thyme**
     1   **pound (450g) minced beef**
     1   **tablespoon cooking oil**
     8   **ounces (225g) packaged spaghetti *or***
         ¾ recipe Parsley Pasta, cut into
         linguine (see pages 73 and 69)

For sauce, slice mushrooms and chop green pepper and onion (see photo 1). In a large covered casserole cook mushrooms, green pepper, onion, and garlic in hot butter or margarine until tender. Stir in *undrained* tomatoes, sieved tomatoes, sugar, basil, marjoram, oregano, and ¼ *teaspoon* salt. Bring to boiling. Reduce heat. Simmer, uncovered, for 35 to 40 minutes or to desired consistency, stirring occasionally (see photo 2).

Meanwhile, in a medium mixing bowl combine egg, bread crumbs, parsley, thyme, ¼ teaspoon *salt,* and ⅛ teaspoon *pepper.* Add beef. Mix well. Shape into 1½-inch (4cm) meatballs (see photo 3). In a 10-inch (25.5cm) frying pan cook meatballs in hot oil until brown. Use a slotted spoon to transfer meatballs to tomato mixture. Simmer, uncovered, 10 to 15 minutes more or until meatballs are cooked.

Cook pasta in boiling salted water until al dente (see photos 1–2, page 14). Allow 10 to 12 minutes for packaged spaghetti or 1½ to 2 minutes for Parsley Pasta linguine. Immediately drain. Spoon sauce over pasta (see photo 4). Makes 5 main-dish servings.

1 Cut the mushrooms into thin lengthwise slices. To prepare the onion, peel it, then cut it in half. (For the green pepper, first cut it in half, then discard the seeds and membrane.) To chop, place the onion or green pepper flat side down on a cutting board. Slice the vegetable in one direction. Then, holding the slices together, slice again in the other direction, as shown.

2 Reduce the heat under the boiling sauce, slowing it to a constant simmer. It's simmering when a few bubbles form slowly and burst before they reach the surface, making a plopping noise. This usually occurs just below boiling—between 185°F (85°C) and 210°F (99°C). Stir the sauce occasionally as it simmers to prevent sticking.

3 To shape equal-size 1½-inch (4cm) meatballs, form the meat mixture into a long roll that is 1½ inches (4cm) in diameter. Slice the roll into ¾-inch-thick (2cm) pieces, as shown. Then shape the slices into balls. You should get about 16 meatballs.

4 To serve, spoon the simmered sauce over the hot cooked pasta. Warming the serving plate first will help keep the pasta and sauce hot longer (see tip, page 15).

Spaghetti with Whisky-Cream Sauce

As the vegetables simmer, they absorb the whisky, creating the well-rounded flavour of this rich sauce.

1 medium onion
1 stalk celery
1 ounce (25g) snipped chives
1 clove garlic, minced
3 tablespoons butter *or* margarine
4 fluid ounces (110ml) Scotch whisky *or* bourbon
12 fluid ounces (330ml) whipping cream
6 ounces (175g) spaghetti *or* spaghettini

For sauce, thinly slice onion and chop celery (see photo 1, page 36). In a medium saucepan cook onion, celery, chives, and garlic in hot butter or margarine until tender. Add Scotch whisky or bourbon, ¼ teaspoon *salt,* and ⅛ teaspoon *pepper.* Bring to boiling. Reduce heat. Simmer, *uncovered,* about 12 minutes or until almost all liquid is evaporated, stirring occasionally (see photo 2, page 36). Stir in whipping cream. Cook and stir about 5 minutes or until mixture thickens.

Meanwhile, cook pasta in boiling salted water until al dente (see photos 1–2, page 14). Allow 10 to 12 minutes for spaghetti or 8 to 10 minutes for spaghettini. Immediately drain. Spoon sauce over pasta (see photo 4, page 37). Toss gently. Sprinkle with grated Parmesan cheese, if desired. Makes 4 side-dish servings.

Spicy Fish Sauce

¾ pound (350g) fresh *or* frozen fish fillets
1 green pepper
1 clove garlic, minced
2 tablespoons olive oil *or* cooking oil
15 ounces (425g) tinned sieved tomatoes
1 teaspoon instant chicken bouillon granules
1 teaspoon chilli powder
¼ teaspoon dried basil, crushed
Several drops bottled hot pepper sauce
6 ounces (175g) packaged spaghetti *or* ⅓ recipe Lemon Pasta, cut into linguine (see pages 78 and 69)

Thaw fish, if frozen. Remove any skin and cut fillets into 1-inch (2.5cm) chunks. Set aside.

For sauce, chop green pepper (see photo 1, page 36). In a saucepan cook pepper and garlic in hot olive or cooking oil until tender. Stir in sieved tomatoes, bouillon granules, chilli powder, basil, and hot pepper sauce. Bring to boiling. Reduce heat. Simmer, covered, for 15 minutes, stirring occasionally (see photo 2, page 36). Add fish. Cover and simmer for 8 to 10 minutes or until fish flakes easily when tested with a fork.

Cook pasta in boiling salted water until al dente (see photos 1–2, page 14). Allow 10 to 12 minutes for spaghetti or 1½ to 2 minutes for Lemon linguine. Drain. Spoon sauce over pasta (see photo 4, page 37). Makes 4 main-dish servings.

Is There a Proper Way To Eat Spaghetti?

That question has been argued for years. One school of thought says you should catch a few strands of pasta on a fork. Then, with the tines rested against a large spoon, twist the fork to wrap up the pasta.

Yet others say you should spear a few strands on a fork. Then, with the tip of the fork rested against the plate (*not* a spoon), twirl the fork and pasta.

Our advice? Use whatever works for you.

Fresh Tomato-Herb Sauce

Some fresh tomatoes have more water in them than others. So the time it takes to simmer the sauce down to 12 fluid ounces (330ml) may vary.

1 medium onion
1 tablespoon butter *or* margarine
2 pounds (900g) fresh tomatoes, cut up
   (6 medium)
2 teaspoons snipped fresh marjoram *or*
   ¾ teaspoon dried marjoram, crushed
2 teaspoons snipped fresh basil *or*
   ¾ teaspoon dried basil, crushed
½ teaspoon caster sugar
½ teaspoon salt
6 ounces (175g) packaged rotelle *or*
   ½ recipe Garlic Pasta, shaped into
   mushroom caps (see pages 72 and
   77)

For sauce, chop onion (see photo 1, page 36). In a large saucepan cook chopped onion in hot butter or margarine until tender but not brown. Stir in tomatoes, marjoram, basil, sugar, and salt. Bring to boiling. Reduce heat. Simmer, uncovered, for 30 minutes, stirring occasionally (see photo 2, page 36).

Pass sauce through a food mill or a sieve. Discard skins, seeds, and any other solids. Return sauce to the saucepan. Bring to boiling. Reduce heat. Simmer, uncovered, for 10 to 15 minutes more or until sauce is reduced to 12 fluid ounces (330ml), stirring occasionally.

Cook pasta in boiling salted water until al dente (see photos 1–2, page 14). Allow 8 to 10 minutes for packaged rotelle or 6 to 7 minutes for Garlic Pasta mushroom caps. Immediately drain. Spoon sauce over pasta (see photo 4, page 37). Makes 6 side-dish servings.

Bolognese Sauce Over Pasta

Just like traditional Bolognese sauce, this recipe calls for a combination of meats. For convenience, though, you can use 1 pound (450g) of minced beef and omit the minced pork or veal and the bacon.

1 large onion
1 stick celery
½ of a medium carrot
¾ pound (350g) minced beef
¼ pound (110g) minced pork *or* veal
2 rashers streaky bacon, finely chopped
28 ounces (780g) tinned tomatoes, cut up
6 ounces (175g) tomato puree
4 fluid ounces (110ml) dry white wine
¼ teaspoon salt
⅛ teaspoon ground nutmeg
⅛ teaspoon pepper
8 ounces (225g) packaged spaghetti *or*
   ¾ recipe Oat Pasta, cut into linguine
   (see pages 72 and 69)
3 fluid ounces (75ml) single cream
   Grated Parmesan cheese (optional)

For sauce, chop onion, slice celery, and coarsely chop carrot (see photo 1, page 36). In a large saucepan cook onion, celery, carrot, beef, pork or veal, and bacon until meat is done and vegetables are tender. Drain off fat.

Stir *undrained* tomatoes, tomato puree, wine, salt, nutmeg, and pepper into meat mixture. Bring to boiling. Reduce heat. Simmer, uncovered, 45 to 60 minutes or to desired consistency, stirring occasionally (see photo 2, page 36).

Meanwhile, cook pasta in boiling salted water till al dente (see photos 1–2, page 14). Allow 10 to 12 minutes for packaged spaghetti or 1½ to 2 minutes for Oat Pasta linguine. Immediately drain. Stir cream into sauce. Spoon sauce over pasta (see photo 4, page 37). Pass Parmesan cheese, if desired. Makes 5 main-dish servings.

Marsala Tomato Sauce

Like an extra-robust flavour? Marsala wine does it for this savoury sauce.

2 **rashers streaky bacon, cut into ½-inch (1cm) pieces**
1 **small green pepper**
1 **clove garlic, minced**
15 **ounces (425g) tinned sieved tomatoes**
2 **fluid ounces (55ml) water**
2 **fluid ounces (55ml) dry marsala**
1 **teaspoon caster sugar**
½ **teaspoon dried oregano, crushed**
6 **ounces (175g) packaged linguine *or* ½ recipe Herb Pasta, cut into linguine (see pages 71 and 69)**

In a medium saucepan cook bacon until crisp. Drain on kitchen paper, reserving drippings in saucepan. Crumble bacon and set aside.

For sauce, chop green pepper (see photo 1, page 36). Cook green pepper and garlic in reserved drippings until tender but not brown. Stir in sieved tomatoes, water, marsala, sugar, and oregano. Bring to boiling. Reduce heat. Simmer, uncovered, for 15 to 20 minutes or to desired consistency, stirring occasionally (see photo 2, page 36).

Meanwhile, cook pasta in boiling salted water until al dente (see photos 1–2, page 14). Allow 8 to 10 minutes for packaged linguine or 1½ to 2 minutes for Herb Pasta linguine. Immediately drain. Spoon sauce over pasta (see photo 4, page 37). Sprinkle with crumbled bacon. Makes 4 side-dish servings.

Curried Chicken And Pasta

2 **whole medium chicken breasts (about 1½ pounds [700g] total), skinned, boned, and halved lengthwise**
1 **small onion**
2 **large cloves garlic, minced**
2 **teaspoons curry powder**
1 **ounce (25g) butter *or* margarine**
1 **pound (450g) tinned tomatoes, cut up**
8 **ounces (225g) tinned sieved tomatoes**
1 **teaspoon caster sugar**
½ **teaspoon instant chicken bouillon granules**
1 **medium apple, cored and chopped**
6 **ounces (175g) packaged vermicelli *or* ⅓ recipe Apple Pasta, cut into linguine (see pages 78 and 69)**
2 **ounces (50g) chopped peanuts**
  Snipped parsley (optional)

Rinse chicken, then pat dry. Cut into bite-size strips. Set aside.

For sauce, chop onion (see photo 1, page 36). In a large saucepan cook onion, garlic, and curry powder in hot butter or margarine until onion is tender but not brown. Stir in *undrained* tomatoes, sieved tomatoes, sugar, and bouillon granules. Bring to boiling. Reduce heat. Simmer, uncovered, for 15 minutes, stirring occasionally (see photo 2, page 36). Add chicken and apple. Simmer, uncovered, 8 to 10 minutes more or until chicken is tender enough to be easily pierced with a fork.

Meanwhile, cook pasta in boiling salted water until al dente (see photos 1–2, page 14). Allow 5 to 7 minutes for packaged vermicelli or 1½ to 2 minutes for Apple Pasta linguine. Immediately drain. Spoon sauce over pasta (see photo 4, page 37). Toss gently. Sprinkle with peanuts. Garnish with parsley, if desired. Makes 4 main-dish servings.

Vegetable Medley in Tomato-Wine Sauce

 1 small onion
 1 clove garlic, minced
 1 tablespoon olive oil *or* cooking oil
15 ounces (425g) tinned sieved tomatoes
 2 fluid ounces (110ml) dry red wine
 ½ teaspoon caster sugar
 ½ teaspoon dried basil, crushed
 ¾ pound (350g) loose-pack frozen mixed broccoli, carrots, and cauliflower
 6 ounces (175g) packaged conchiglie *or* ½ recipe Whole Grain Pasta, shaped into mushroom caps (see pages 71 and 77)

For sauce, chop onion (see photo 1, page 36). In a large saucepan cook onion and garlic in hot olive oil or cooking oil until onion is tender but not brown. Stir in sieved tomatoes, wine, sugar, basil, and ⅛ teaspoon *salt*. Bring to boiling. Reduce heat. Simmer, covered, for 20 minutes, stirring occasionally (see photo 2, page 36).

Place broccoli, carrots, and cauliflower in a colander. Run warm water over vegetables to thaw. Add vegetables to sauce. Cover; simmer 6 to 8 minutes more or until vegetables are tender.

Meanwhile, cook pasta in boiling salted water until al dente (see photos 1–2, page 14). Allow 12 to 14 minutes for conchiglie or 6 to 7 minutes for Whole Grain Pasta mushroom caps. Immediately drain. Spoon sauce over pasta (see photo 4, page 37). Makes 5 side-dish servings.

Rich Mushroom-And-Wine Linguine

Simmering the sauce deliciously concentrates the mellow wine flavour in the mushrooms.

 6 ounces (175g) fresh mushrooms
 7 medium spring onions
 1 ounce (25g) butter *or* margarine
 4 fluid ounces (110ml) dry white wine
 1½ teaspoons snipped fresh basil *or* ½ teaspoon dried basil, crushed
 ¼ teaspoon salt
 6 fluid ounces (165ml) whipping cream
 4 ounces (110g) packaged egg *or* whole wheat linguine, *or* ¼ recipe Tomato-Herb Pasta, cut into linguine (see pages 79 and 69)

For sauce, slice mushrooms and spring onions (see photo 1, page 36). In a medium saucepan cook mushrooms and onions in hot butter or margarine until tender. Stir in wine, basil, and salt. Bring to boiling. Reduce heat. Simmer, uncovered, for 15 minutes or until the liquid is reduced to 2 to 4 tablespoons, stirring occasionally (see photo 2, page 36). Stir in whipping cream. Cook and stir about 5 minutes or until mixture thickens.

Meanwhile, cook pasta in boiling salted water until al dente (see photos 1–2, page 14). Allow 8 to 10 minutes for packaged linguine or 1½ to 2 minutes for Tomato-Herb Pasta linguine. Immediately drain. Spoon sauce over pasta (see photo 4, page 37). Makes 6 side-dish servings.

Creamy Pasta Dishes

Put cooked pasta together with a white sauce, and the possibilities are endless!

We started with this pasta-and-sauce base and then added a variety of ingredients to create these sensational dishes.

First try our versions of all your favourite pasta casseroles. Then try our unique creations.

Either way, you'll find dishes here that will delight your palate.

Sherried Veal

Sherried Veal

Melt-in-your-mouth veal and a velvety sherried cream sauce make an elegant, sumptuous dish.

1 to 2 ounces (25 to 50g) butter *or*
    margarine
1 pound (450g) veal escalope, cut into
    thin bite-size strips
1 ounce (25g) butter *or* margarine
2 medium carrots, thinly sliced
3 spring onions, sliced into 1-inch
    (2.5cm) pieces
3 tablespoons plain flour
½ teaspoon salt
¼ teaspoon freshly ground black pepper
18 fluid ounces (500ml) single cream *or*
    milk
1 ounce (25g) sliced stoned ripe olives
2 fluid ounces (55ml) dry sherry
8 ounces (225g) packaged linguine *or* ½
    recipe Pasta Verde, cut into linguine
    (see pages 76 and 69)
    Parsley sprigs

1 Cook the vegetables in the hot butter or margarine until they are tender, but not brown. Then stir in the flour and seasonings with a wooden spoon until no lumps remain.

In a 10-inch (25.5cm) frying pan melt *1 ounce (25g)* butter or margarine. Add *half* of the veal. Stir-fry until brown. Remove from pan; set aside. Repeat with rest of veal. Add another *1 ounce (25g)* butter or margarine, if necessary.

Add 1 ounce (25g) butter or margarine to pan; stir until melted. Add carrots and onions; cook in hot butter or margarine for 3 to 4 minutes or until tender. Stir in flour, salt, and pepper (see photo 1). Add single cream or milk all at once (see photo 2). Cook and stir until thickened and bubbly, then cook and stir 1 minute more (see photo 3). Stir in cooked veal, sliced olives, and sherry (see photo 4). Heat through. Snip parsley (see photo 5).

2 Add the milk, cream, or other liquid all at once to the flour-butter mixture. Then stir with a wooden spoon or wire whisk to distribute the flour-butter mixture evenly throughout the liquid.

Meanwhile, cook pasta in boiling salted water until al dente (see photos 1–2, page 14). Allow 8 to 10 minutes for packaged linguine or 1½ to 2 minutes for Pasta Verde linguine. Immediately drain. Spoon veal mixture over hot linguine. Sprinkle with snipped parsley. Serve immediately. Makes 4 main-dish servings.

3 Cook and stir continuously over medium heat until the mixture thickens and bubbles form across the entire surface. Stir with a gentle figure-eight motion so the mixture heats evenly. Cook 1 minute longer to make sure the flour is cooked and the sauce does not taste starchy.

4 When the sauce is cooked, add the remaining ingredients.

5 The easiest way to snip parsley or other fresh herbs is in a measuring jug. Place the fresh herb in the jug and use kitchen scissors to snip it finely, as shown.

Herb 'n' Garlic Courgette and Pasta

1 small courgette, halved lengthwise and thinly sliced
2 cloves garlic, minced
1 ounce (25g) butter *or* margarine
2 teaspoons plain flour
¾ teaspoon dried basil, crushed
¼ teaspoon salt
 Dash pepper
6 fluid ounces (165ml) milk
4 ounces (110g) packaged fettuccine *or* spaghetti, *or* ⅓ recipe Corn Pasta, cut into fettuccine (see pages 70 and 69)

For sauce, in a saucepan cook courgette and garlic in hot butter or margarine 2 to 3 minutes or until courgette is crisp but tender. Stir in flour, basil, salt, and pepper (see photo 1, page 44). Add milk all at once (see photo 2, page 44). Cook and stir until thick and bubbly, then cook and stir 1 minute more (see photo 3, page 45).

Meanwhile, cook pasta in boiling salted water until al dente (see photos 1–2, page 14). Allow 8 to 10 minutes for packaged fettuccine, 10 to 12 minutes for packaged spaghetti, or 1½ to 2 minutes for Corn Pasta fettuccine. Immediately drain. Spoon sauce over hot pasta. Toss gently. Serve immediately. Makes 6 side-dish servings.

Creamy Walnut Pasta

2 ounces (50g) coarsely chopped walnuts
½ ounce (10g) butter *or* margarine
2 spring onions, sliced
2 teaspoons plain flour
¼ teaspoon salt
⅛ teaspoon freshly ground black pepper
½ pint (275ml) milk
2 ounces (50g) garlic and herb cream cheese
4 ounces (110g) packaged spinach noodles *or* ¼ recipe Pasta Verde, cut into fettuccine (see pages 76 and 69)

For sauce, in a medium saucepan cook walnuts in hot butter or margarine over medium-high heat for 1 minute. Add onion. Cook and stir 1 to 2 minutes more or until walnuts are golden brown. Stir in flour, salt, and pepper (see photo 1, page 44). Add milk all at once (see photo 2, page 44). Cook and stir until slightly thick and bubbly, then cook and stir 1 minute more (see photo 3, page 45). Stir in cheese until melted.

Meanwhile, cook pasta in boiling salted water until al dente (see photos 1–2, page 14). Allow 6 to 8 minutes for spinach noodles or 1½ to 2 minutes for Pasta Verde fettuccine. Immediately drain. Spoon sauce over hot pasta. Toss gently. Makes 4 side-dish servings.

Measuring Dry and Cooked Pasta

If you don't have a kitchen scale, it's nice to know some cup measurements for pasta.
● Four ounces of uncooked **elbow macaroni** or **conchiglie** measures about 1 cup. When it's cooked, you'll have approximately 2½ cups of pasta.

● Four ounces of uncooked **medium noodles** measures about 3 cups. When it's cooked, you'll have about 3 cups of pasta.
● Four ounces of uncooked 10-inch-long **spaghetti** held together in a bunch has about a 1-inch diameter. When it's cooked, you'll have about 2 cups of pasta.

Soured Cream- and Prawn-Sauced Pasta

6   ounces (175g) sliced fresh mushrooms
1   ounce (25g) butter *or* margarine
2   tablespoons plain flour
¼   teaspoon salt
¼   teaspoon dried tarragon, crushed
⅛   teaspoon pepper
½   pint (275ml) milk
4   ounces (110g) soured cream
8   ounces (225g) frozen cooked prawns, thawed and drained
2   tablespoons dry white wine
    Parsley sprigs
6   ounces (175g) packaged fettuccine *or* ½ recipe Parsley Pasta, cut into fettuccine (see pages 73 and 69)

In a medium saucepan cook mushrooms in hot butter or margarine until tender. Stir in flour, salt, tarragon, and pepper (see photo 1, page 44). Add milk all at once (see photo 2, page 44). Cook and stir until thickened and bubbly, then cook and stir 1 minute more (see photo 3, page 45). Gradually stir about ¼ *pint (150ml)* of the hot mixture into soured cream; return to saucepan, mixing well. Stir in prawns and wine (see photo 4, page 45). Heat through; *do not boil.* Snip parsley; set aside (see photo 5, page 45).

Meanwhile, cook pasta in boiling salted water until al dente (see photos 1–2, page 14). Allow 8 to 10 minutes for packaged fettuccine or 1½ to 2 minutes for Parsley Pasta fettuccine. Immediately drain. Spoon prawn mixture over hot pasta. Sprinkle with snipped parsley. Serve immediately. Makes 4 main-dish servings.

Blue Cheese Fettuccine

Are you a blue cheese lover? If so, you may want to sprinkle more crumbled blue cheese on top.

1   ounce (25g) butter *or* margarine
1   tablespoon plain flour
¼   teaspoon salt
    Dash pepper
8   fluid ounces (220ml) milk
2   ounces (50g) soured cream
1   ounce (25g) crumbled blue cheese
1   ounce (25g) sliced stoned black olives
6   ounces (175g) packaged spinach fettuccine *or* ⅓ recipe Pasta Verde, cut into fettuccine (see pages 76 and 69)

For sauce, in a small saucepan melt butter or margarine. Stir in flour, salt, and pepper (see photo 1, page 44). Add milk all at once (see photo 2, page 44). Cook and stir until thickened, then cook and stir 1 minute more (see photo 3, page 45). Gradually stir about ¼ *pint (150ml)* of the hot mixture into soured cream. Reduce heat to low. Return soured cream mixture to saucepan, mixing well. Stir in blue cheese and olives until cheese is nearly melted; *do not boil.*

Meanwhile, cook pasta in boiling salted water until al dente (see photos 1–2, page 14). Allow 8 to 10 minutes for packaged fettuccine or 1½ to 2 minutes for Pasta Verde fettuccine. Immediately drain. Spoon sauce over hot pasta. Toss gently. Makes 6 side-dish servings.

Microwave Directions: (See tip, page 10.) For sauce, in a 2½-pint (1.4l) nonmetal casserole micro-cook butter or margarine, uncovered, on 100% power (HIGH) 30 to 45 seconds or until melted. Stir in flour, salt, and pepper (see photo 1, page 44). Add milk all at once (see photo 2, page 44). Cook, uncovered, for 3 to 5 minutes more or until mixture is thickened and bubbly, stirring after each minute (see photo 3, page 45). Stir in soured cream, cheese, and olives. Cook for 30 seconds. Stir until cheese is nearly melted. Meanwhile, on the *stove-top,* cook pasta as directed above. Immediately drain. Spoon sauce over hot pasta. Toss gently.

Curried Turkey Spaghetti

Feeling adventurous? Explore a different pasta shape by making this recipe with orzo, if you can find it. It's a ricelike pasta that's sometimes called rosamarina.

 1 **small apple, cored and chopped**
 1 **tablespoon curry powder**
 2 **ounces (50g) butter *or* margarine**
 3 **tablespoons plain flour**
 1 **teaspoon instant chicken bouillon granules**
18 **fluid ounces (500ml) milk**
10 **ounces (275g) chopped cooked turkey**
 2 **tablespoons chopped chutney**
 8 **ounces (225g) packaged spaghetti *or* orzo, *or* ⅔ recipe Nut Pasta, cut into linguine (see pages 79 and 69)**
 1 **ounce (25g) peanuts**
 1 **ounce (25g) raisins**
    Chopped chutney (optional)

In a medium saucepan cook apple and curry powder in hot butter or margarine for 1 to 2 minutes. Stir in flour and bouillon granules (see photo 1, page 44). Add milk all at once (see photo 2, page 44). Cook and stir until thickened and bubbly, then cook and stir 1 minute more (see photo 3, page 45). Stir in turkey and 2 tablespoons chutney (see photo 4, page 45). Heat mixture through.

Meanwhile, cook pasta in boiling salted water until al dente (see photos 1–2, page 14). Allow 10 to 12 minutes for packaged spaghetti, 5 to 8 minutes for orzo, or 1½ to 2 minutes for Nut Pasta linguine. Immediately drain. Spoon turkey mixture over hot pasta. Toss gently. Sprinkle with peanuts and raisins. If desired, garnish with additional chutney. Serve immediately. Makes 5 main-dish servings.

Ham-Pasta Bake

For a "change of shape," make this creamy family casserole with conchiglie (medium pasta shells).

3 **ounces (75g) macaroni *or* conchiglie**
2 **ounces (50g) chopped onion**
1 **clove garlic, minced**
1 **ounce (25g) butter *or* margarine**
2 **tablespoons plain flour**
½ **teaspoon dried marjoram, crushed**
8 **fluid ounces (220ml) milk**
4 **ounces (110g) grated Swiss cheese**
3 **ounces (75g) cooked ham, cubed**
5 **ounces (150g) frozen broccoli spears, thawed and chopped**
½ **ounce (10g) soft breadcrumbs**
½ **ounce (10g) butter *or* margarine, melted**

Cook pasta in boiling salted water until al dente (see photos 1–2, page 14). Allow 10 minutes for macaroni or 12 to 14 minutes for conchiglie. Immediately drain. Return pasta to the pan it was cooked in.

Meanwhile, cook onion and garlic in 1 ounce (25g) hot butter or margarine until tender. Stir in flour and marjoram (see photo 1, page 44). Add milk all at once (see photo 2, page 44). Cook and stir until thickened and bubbly (see photo 3, page 45). Stir in cheese until melted. Stir in cooked pasta, ham, and broccoli (see photo 4, page 45). Transfer to a 1¾-pint (1l) casserole. Toss together breadcrumbs and ½ ounce (10g) melted butter or margarine. Sprinkle atop casserole. Bake in a 350°F (180°C) gas mark 4 oven about 40 minutes or until heated through. Makes 3 main-dish servings.

Pasta with Four-Cheese and Vegetable Sauce

Here's the perfect recipe for special occasions. You can even start making it the day before by cutting up the vegetables, meat, and cheeses.

2   **medium carrots, cut into julienne strips**
1   **medium courgette, cut into julienne strips**
½   **pound (225g) fresh mushrooms, quartered**
2   **cloves garlic, minced**
1   **ounce (25g) butter *or* margarine**
2   **tablespoons plain flour**
½   **pint (275ml) milk**
4   **ounces (110g) cream cheese, cut up**
4   **ounces (110g) Brie cheese (rind trimmed), cubed**
4   **ounces (110g) grated Gruyère cheese**
2   **ounces (50g) grated Parmesan cheese**
2   **fluid ounces (55ml) dry white wine**
2   **tablespoons snipped fresh chives**
10   **ounces (275g) packaged linguine *or* 1 recipe Egg Pasta, cut into linguine (see pages 68–69)**
4   **ounces (110g) prosciutto, cut into julienne strips**
  Grated Parmesan cheese (optional)

In a medium saucepan cook carrots in a small amount of boiling water, covered, for 5 minutes. Add courgette. Cook, covered, 3 to 5 minutes more or until crisp-tender. Drain. Keep warm.

For sauce, in a medium saucepan cook mushrooms and garlic in hot butter or margarine until tender. Stir in flour (see photo 1, page 44). Add milk all at once (see photo 2, page 44). Cook and stir until thickened and bubbly (see photo 3, page 45). Stir in cream cheese, Brie cheese, Gruyère cheese, Parmesan cheese, wine, and chives (see photo 4, page 45). Cook and stir over low heat until cheeses melt.

Meanwhile, break or cut pasta into 3- or 4-inch (7.5 or 10cm) pieces. Cook pasta in boiling salted water until al dente (see photos 1–2, page 14). Allow 8 to 10 minutes for packaged linguine or 1½ to 2 minutes for Egg Pasta linguine.

Immediately drain. Spoon sauce over hot pasta. Add cooked carrots and courgette mixture and prosciutto; toss gently. Sprinkle with additional Parmesan cheese, if desired. Serve immediately. Makes 6 main-dish servings.

Macaroni and Cheese Special

Rotelle is also called corkscrew or spiral macaroni.

6   **ounces (175g) macaroni *or* rotelle**
10   **ounces (275g) frozen mixed vegetables**
2   **ounces (50g) chopped onion**
1   **ounce (25g) butter *or* margarine**
2   **tablespoons plain flour**
¼   **teaspoon salt**
⅛   **teaspoon ground red pepper**
16   **fluid ounces (440ml) milk**
8   **ounces (225g) mild cheddar cheese, cubed**
1   **medium tomato, sliced**
2   **tablespoons grated Parmesan cheese**

Cook pasta and vegetables in boiling salted water until pasta is al dente (see photos 1–2, page 14). Allow 10 minutes for macaroni or 8 to 10 minutes for rotelle. Immediately drain. Return mixture to the pan it was cooked in.

Meanwhile, in a medium saucepan cook onion in hot butter or margarine until tender. Stir in flour, salt, and red pepper (see photo 1, page 44). Add milk all at once (see photo 2, page 44). Cook and stir until thickened and bubbly (see photo 3, page 45). Stir in cheddar cheese until melted. Stir in cooked pasta and vegetables (see photo 4, page 45). Transfer to a 3¼-pint (1.75l) casserole. Arrange tomato slices atop mixture. Sprinkle with Parmesan cheese. Bake in a 350°F (180°C) gas mark 4 oven for 30 to 35 minutes or until heated through. Makes 6 main-dish servings.

Pasta With Pesto

Looking for relief from humdrum meals? Let pesto break your taste bud barrier.

Every bite of this zesty oil-herb puree bursts with flavour. Toss some with your favourite pasta and presto—you've created a taste sensation!

Fettuccine with Fresh Pesto

Fettuccine with Fresh Pesto

*Traditionally, pesto is made with a mortar and pestle.
Our modern version uses a food processor or blender,
cutting the preparation time by more than half.*

**2 bunches fresh basil, stems removed
2 cloves garlic
3 ounces (75g) grated Parmesan cheese
4 fluid ounces (110ml) olive oil *or*
      cooking oil
6 ounces (175g) packaged fettuccine *or*
      ½ recipe Nut Pasta, cut into
      fettuccine (see pages 79 and 69)**

For pesto, in a food processor bowl or blender
container combine basil leaves and garlic. Cover
and process or blend until finely chopped and
well combined. Stop the processor or blender
several times and scrape the sides (see photo 1).

Add Parmesan cheese to basil-garlic mixture.
Process or blend until combined (see photo 2).

Add olive oil or cooking oil a little at a time, processing or blending well after each addition (see
photo 3). Mixture will be thick.

Cook pasta in boiling salted water until al dente
(see photos 1–2, page 14). Allow 8 to 10 minutes for packaged fettuccine or 1½ to 2 minutes
for Nut Pasta fettuccine. Immediately drain. Return pasta to the pan it was cooked in. Add a
third of the pesto. Toss until pasta is well coated. If desired, garnish with basil leaves. Serve
immediately. Makes 4 side-dish servings.

Note: Divide remaining pesto in half. Freeze in
two 4-ounce (110g) freezer containers. To
serve, thaw and bring to room temperature.
Toss with hot cooked pasta as above, spoon
over hot cooked vegetables, or stir into soup.

1 Stop the food pro-
cessor or blender
several times and scrape
the sides of the contain-
er or bowl with a rubber
spatula. Some of the
herb and garlic will be
whirled out of reach
of the cutting blades.
Scraping the sides
pushes these pieces
back in range of the
blades, allowing for an
evenly chopped mixture.

2 Add the Parmesan
cheese to the pu-
reed herb-garlic mixture.
Process or blend until
well combined. The mix-
ture will appear some-
what grainy, as shown.

3 Add the oil a little at
a time. If you're us-
ing a food processor,
add it in a very thin
stream through the pro-
cessor's feed tube, as
shown. For a blender,
add the oil in a very
thin stream through the
opening in the lid. (If
your blender doesn't
have this opening, place
the lid slightly ajar.)

   Process or blend well
after each addition.
Stop and scrape the
sides of the container,
as necessary. Adding
just a little oil at a time
lets the oil work slowly
into the herb-garlic mix-
ture and forms a better
bond. The mixture
should be smoother
than it was after the ad-
dition of the cheese and
about the consistency of
very thick mayonnaise.

Parsley-Based Pesto

This version uses easy-to-find parsley rather than fresh basil. It has a wonderful, full flavour.

2 **bunches parsley with stems removed**
1 **tablespoon dried basil, crushed**
2 **cloves garlic**
3 **ounces (75g) grated Parmesan cheese**
4 **fluid ounces (110ml) olive oil *or* cooking oil**
6 **ounces (175g) packaged medium noodles *or* ⅓ recipe Carrot Pasta, cut into noodles (see pages 78 and 69)**

For pesto, in a food processor bowl or blender container combine parsley, dried basil, and garlic. Cover and process or blend until finely chopped and well combined. Stop the processor or blender several times and scrape the sides (see photo 1).

Add Parmesan cheese to parsley-garlic mixture. Process or blend until combined (see photo 2).

Add olive oil or cooking oil a little at a time, processing or blending well after each addition (see photo 3). Mixture will be thick.

Cook the pasta in boiling salted water until al dente (see photos 1–2, page 14). Allow 6 to 8 minutes for packaged noodles or 1½ to 2 minutes for Carrot Pasta noodles. Immediately drain. Return the pasta to the pan it was cooked in. Add a *third* of the pesto. Toss until the pasta is well coated. Serve immediately. Makes 4 side-dish servings.

Note: Divide remaining pesto in half. Freeze in two 4-ounce (110g) freezer containers. To serve, thaw and bring to room temperature. Toss with hot cooked pasta as above, spoon over hot cooked vegetables, or stir into soup.

Layers Of Pasta

When you're *really* hungry, hardly anything satisfies that hearty appetite like layer upon layer of pasta, sauce, and cheese.

The classic Italian version of lasagne immediately comes to mind as king of these layered wonders. But we've also created many others, including Greek and Mexican spin-offs. Our variations on the lasagne theme will make your taste buds clamour for more.

Classic Lasagne

Classic Lasagne

Let the lasagne stand for 10 minutes after baking so it will set up and hold a cut edge when served.

¼	**pound (110g) pork sausage meat**
3	**ounces (75g) sliced fresh mushrooms**
3	**ounces (75g) chopped onion**
1	**clove garlic, minced**
16	**ounces (450g) tinned tomatoes, cut up**
15	**ounces (425g) tinned sieved tomatoes**
1	**teaspoon caster sugar**
1	**teaspoon dried basil, crushed**
1	**teaspoon dried oregano, crushed**
½	**teaspoon celery salt**
1	**beaten egg**
8	**ounces (225g) ricotta *or* cottage cheese, drained**
1	**ounce (25g) grated Parmesan cheese**
6	**packaged lasagne strips *or* ⅓ recipe Egg Pasta (see page 68)**
4	**ounces (110g) grated mozzarella cheese**
1	**ounce (25g) grated Parmesan cheese**

For sauce, in a saucepan cook sausage, mushrooms, onion, and garlic until sausage is brown and onion is tender. Drain fat. Stir in *undrained* tomatoes, sieved tomatoes, sugar, basil, oregano, celery salt, and ⅛ teaspoon *pepper*. Bring to boiling. Reduce heat and simmer, uncovered, for 35 to 40 minutes or to desired consistency.

Meanwhile, in a small mixing bowl stir together egg, ricotta or cottage cheese, and 1 ounce (25g) Parmesan cheese. Set aside.

If using Egg Pasta, on a lightly floured surface roll the dough into a 15x10-inch (36x25.5cm) rectangle ¹⁄₁₆ to ⅛ inch (1.5mm to 3mm) thick. (*Or,* if using a pasta machine, pass dough through until it reaches desired thickness. Cut dough into six 10x2½-inch (25.5x6cm) strips (see tip, right).

Cook pasta in boiling salted water until *almost* al dente (see photo 1). Allow 8 to 9 minutes for packaged lasagne or 1 to 1½ minutes for Egg Pasta lasagne. Immediately drain. Rinse with cold water; drain well.

Arrange 3 lasagne strips in a greased 10x6x2-inch (25.5x15x5cm) baking dish. Trim to fit. Spread with *half* of the ricotta cheese mixture (see photo 2). Spoon *half* of the sauce over top (see photo 3). Sprinkle with *half* of the mozzarella cheese. Repeat layers of lasagne, cheese mixture, and sauce; reserve remaining mozzarella. Sprinkle 1 ounce (25g) Parmesan cheese over all. Bake, covered, in a 350°F (180°C) gas mark 4 oven for 35 minutes. Uncover and sprinkle remaining mozzarella on top (see photo 4). Bake 5 to 10 minutes more or until heated through. Let stand for 10 minutes before serving. Makes 6 main-dish servings.

1 Cook the pasta for the time indicated in the recipe. Pasta boiled this amount of time will be *almost* al dente. The pasta finishes cooking as the casserole bakes.

2 Spread *half* of the cheese-egg mixture over the lasagne. The egg makes the cheese easier to spread.

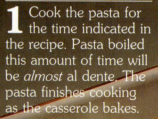

4 Sprinkle the final cheese layer on top during the last part of the baking time. This allows the cheese to melt but remain attractive.

3 Spoon *half* of the sauce atop the cheese-egg layer. Use the back of the spoon to spread it in an even layer over the cheese.

Making Lasagne

For lasagne, cut the rolled dough into 10x2½- inch (25.5x5cm) strips with a fluted pastry wheel or a sharp knife, as shown.

For mafaldine, which are narrower than lasagne, cut the rolled-out dough into 10x¾-inch (25.5x2cm) strips.

Place any remaining dough in a polythene bag. Chill it to be re-rolled for another use.

Chicken Lasagne

Our editors think this creamy, mild-flavoured lasagne is a pleasant change from traditional spicy versions.

6 packaged lasagne strips *or* ¼ recipe Tomato-Herb Pasta (see page 79)
10 ounces (275g) frozen chopped spinach *or* 16 ounces (450g) fresh spinach, coarsely chopped
1 beaten egg
4 ounces (110g) cottage cheese
⅛ teaspoon pepper
2 spring onions, sliced
2 cloves garlic, minced
3 tablespoons butter *or* margarine
3 tablespoons plain flour
1½ teaspoons instant chicken bouillon granules
¼ teaspoon ground nutmeg
12 fluid ounces (330ml) milk
7 ounces (200g) chopped cooked chicken
4 ounces (110g) grated Swiss cheese

If using Tomato-Herb Pasta, on a lightly floured surface roll the dough into a 15x10-inch (36x25.5cm) rectangle ¹⁄₁₆ to ⅛ inch (1.5mm to 3mm) thick. (*Or,* if using a pasta machine, pass dough through until it reaches the desired thickness.) Cut dough into six 10x2½-inch (25.5x6cm) strips (see tip, page 57).

Cook pasta in boiling salted water until *almost* al dente (see photo 1, page 56). Allow 8 to 9 minutes for packaged lasagne or 1 to 1½ minutes for Tomato-Herb lasagne. Immediately drain. Rinse with cold water, then drain well. Set lasagne aside.

Meanwhile, cook frozen spinach according to the package directions. (*Or,* in a large saucepan cook fresh spinach, covered, in a small amount of water. Reduce heat when steam forms. Cook 3 to 5 minutes or until done, turning frequently with a fork.) Drain well. In a medium mixing bowl stir together egg, cottage cheese, and pepper. Stir in spinach. Set aside.

For sauce, in a small saucepan cook spring onion and garlic in hot butter or margarine until tender. Stir in flour, bouillon granules, and nutmeg. Add milk all at once. Cook and stir until thickened and bubbly. Remove from heat.

Arrange 3 cooked strips of lasagne in a well-greased 10x6x2-inch (25.5x15x5cm) baking dish. Trim to fit. Place *half* of the chicken on top. Spread with *half* of the spinach-cheese mixture (see photo 2, page 56). Spoon *half* of the sauce over top (see photo 3, page 57). Sprinkle with *half* of the Swiss cheese. Repeat layers of lasagne, chicken, spinach-cheese mixture, and sauce; reserve remaining Swiss cheese. Bake, covered, in a 350°F (180°C) gas mark 4 oven for 30 minutes. Uncover and sprinkle remaining Swiss cheese on top (see photo 4, page 57). Bake 5 to 10 minutes more or until heated through. Let stand for 10 minutes before serving. Makes 6 main-dish servings.

Meatless Courgette Lasagne

You won't miss the meat in this satisfying main dish.

2 medium courgettes
2 beaten eggs
16 ounces (450g) ricotta cheese *or* cottage cheese
1 ounce (25g) snipped parsley
6 packaged lasagne strips *or* ¼ recipe Tomato-Herb Pasta (see page 79)
16 ounces (450g) meatless spaghetti sauce
4 ounces (110g) grated Muenster cheese

Cut courgettes *lengthwise* into ¼-inch-wide (.5cm) slices. In a large saucepan cook courgettes in a small amount of salted water about 5 minutes or until crisp-tender. Drain well.

In a medium mixing bowl stir together eggs, ricotta or cottage cheese, and parsley. Set aside.

If using Tomato-Herb Pasta, on a lightly floured surface roll the dough into a 15x10-inch (36x25.5cm) rectangle ¹⁄₁₆ to ⅛ inch (1.5mm to 3mm) thick. (*Or,* if using a pasta machine, pass the dough through until it reaches desired thickness.) Cut dough into six 10x2½-inch (25.5x6cm) strips (*see tip, page 57*).

Cook pasta in boiling salted water until *almost* al dente (*see photo 1, page 56*). Allow 8 to 9 minutes for packaged lasagne or 1 to 1½ minutes for Tomato-Herb lasagne. Immediately drain. Rinse with cold water; drain well.

Arrange 3 strips of lasagne in a greased 10x6x2-inch (25.5x15x5cm) baking dish. Trim to fit. Place *half* of the courgettes on top. Spread with *half* of the ricotta cheese mixture (*see photo 2, page 56*). Spoon *half* of the spaghetti sauce over top (*see photo 3, page 57*). Sprinkle with *half* of the Muenster cheese. Repeat layers of lasagne, courgettes, ricotta cheese mixture, and sauce; reserve remaining cheese. Bake, covered, in a 350°F (180°C) gas mark 4 oven for 30 minutes. Sprinkle remaining cheese on top (*see photo 4, page 57*). Bake 5 to 10 minutes more or until heated through. Let stand for 10 minutes before serving. Makes 6 main-dish servings.

Lamb and Feta Layered Casserole

The meat, sauce, cheeses, and seasonings in this hearty dish are inspired by Greek cooking.

1 pound (450g) minced lamb *or* beef
3 spring onions, sliced
1 pint (570ml) prepared sieved tomatoes
½ teaspoon ground cinnamon
1 beaten egg
5 ounces (150g) crumbled feta cheese
6 fluid ounces (165ml) cottage cheese
3 tablespoons snipped parsley
1 teaspoon dried oregano, crushed
6 packaged lasagne strips *or* ¼ recipe Pasta Verde (see page 76)
1 ounce (25g) sliced stoned black olives

For sauce, in a 10-inch (25.5cm) frying pan cook lamb or beef and spring onion until meat is brown. Drain off fat. Stir in sieved tomatoes and cinnamon. Set aside.

Meanwhile, in a small mixing bowl stir together egg, *3 ounces (75g)* of the feta cheese, cottage cheese, parsley, and oregano. Set aside.

If using Pasta Verde, on a lightly floured surface roll the dough into a 15x10-inch (38x25.5cm) rectangle ¹⁄₁₆ to ⅛ inch (1.5 to 3mm) thick. (*Or,* if using a pasta machine, pass the dough through until ¹⁄₁₆ to ⅛ inch [1.5 to 3mm] thick.) Cut into six 10x2½-inch (25.5x6cm) strips (*see tip, page 57*).

Cook pasta in boiling salted water until *almost* al dente (*see photo 1, page 56*). Allow 8 to 9 minutes for packaged lasagne or 1 to 1½ minutes for Pasta Verde lasagne. Immediately drain. Rinse with cold water; drain well.

Arrange 3 strips of lasagne in a greased 10x6x2-inch (25.5x15x5cm) baking dish. Trim to fit. Spread with *half* of the feta cheese mixture (*see photo 2, page 56*). Spoon *half* of the sauce over top (*see photo 3, page 57*). Repeat layers of lasagne, cheese mixture, and sauce. Bake, covered, in a 350°F (180°C) gas mark 4 oven for 50 to 55 minutes or until heated through. Garnish with olives and remaining feta cheese. Let stand for 10 minutes. Makes 6 main-dish servings.

Aubergine Mafaldine Parmigiana

If you like, use packaged lasagne instead of mafaldine.

1 **medium aubergine, peeled and cut crosswise into ½-inch (1cm) slices**
1 **beaten egg**
3 **ounces (75g) fine dry breadcrumbs**
2 **to 4 fluid ounces (55 to 110ml) olive oil *or* cooking oil**
14 **packaged mafaldine strips *or* ¼ recipe Whole Grain Pasta (see page 71) Snappy Tomato Sauce *or* 1¼ pints (720ml) tinned Bolognese sauce**
4 **slices mozzarella cheese (6 ounces [175g])**
1 **ounce (25g) grated Parmesan cheese**

Dip aubergine into egg, then into breadcrumbs, turning to coat well. In a 10-inch (25.5cm) frying pan cook *half* of the aubergine slices in 2 fluid ounces (55ml) hot olive oil or cooking oil about 3 minutes on each side or until brown. Add additional oil to the pan as necessary. Drain well on kitchen paper. Repeat with remaining aubergine. Set aside.

If using Whole Grain Pasta, on lightly floured surface roll dough into 12x10-inch (30x25.5cm) rectangle ¹⁄₁₆ to ⅛ inch (1.5 to 3mm) thick. (*Or,* if using a pasta machine, pass dough through until ¹⁄₁₆ to ⅛ inch [1.5 to 3 mm thick].) Cut dough into sixteen 10x¾-inch (25.5x2cm) strips (see tip, page 57).

Cook pasta in boiling salted water until *almost* al dente (see photo 1, page 56). Allow 8 to 9 minutes for packaged mafaldine strips or 1 to 1½ minutes for Whole Grain Pasta mafaldine. Immediately drain. Rinse with cold water, then drain well.

Arrange *half* of the mafaldine in a greased 10x6x2-inch (25.5x15x5cm) baking dish. Trim to fit. Place *half* of the aubergine slices on top, cutting slices to fit. Spoon *half* of the Snappy Tomato Sauce or Bolognese sauce over top (see photo 3, page 57). Top with *half* of the mozzarella cheese. Sprinkle with *half* of the Parmesan cheese. Repeat layers of noodles, aubergine slices, and tomato sauce; reserve remaining mozzarella cheese and Parmesan cheese.

Bake, covered, in a 350°F (180°C) gas mark 4 oven for 35 minutes. Uncover. Sprinkle remaining mozzarella cheese and Parmesan cheese on top (see photo 4, page 57). Bake 5 to 10 minutes more or until heated through. Let stand 10 minutes. Makes 6 main-dish servings.

Snappy Tomato Sauce: In a large saucepan cook ½ pound (225g) *minced pork* until brown. Drain fat. Add three 8-ounce (225g) tins of *sieved tomatoes;* 1 teaspoon *sugar;* 1 teaspoon dried *oregano,* crushed; ½ teaspoon *onion salt;* and ¼ teaspoon *garlic powder.* Bring to boiling. Reduce heat, then simmer, uncovered, for 5 minutes, stirring occasionally. Makes about 1¼ pints (720ml).

Fiesta Pasta

4 **ounces (110g) chopped green pepper**
3 **spring onions, sliced**
2 **ounces (50g) butter *or* margarine**
2 **ounces (50g) plain flour**
½ **teaspoon ground coriander**
½ **pint (275ml) chicken stock**
8 **ounces (225g) soured cream**
2 **tablespoons plain flour**
8 **ounces (225g) chopped cooked chicken**
4 **ounces (110g) green chilli peppers, diced**
16 **packaged mafaldine strips *or* ⅓ recipe Corn Pasta (see page 70)**
6 **ounces (175g) grated cheddar cheese**
2 **ounces (50g) shredded lettuce**
1 **ounce (25g) coarsely crushed chilli-flavoured crisps**
1 **ounce (25g) sliced stoned black olives**
1 **small tomato, chopped**

For sauce, in a medium saucepan cook green pepper, chilli peppers, and spring onion in hot butter or margarine until tender. Stir in 2 ounces (50g) flour and coriander. Add chicken stock all at once. Cook and stir until thickened and bubbly. Remove from heat. Stir together soured cream and 2 tablespoons flour. Stir ¼ pint *(150ml)* of the hot mixture into soured cream mixture; return to saucepan. Stir in chicken. Set aside while preparing pasta.

If using Corn Pasta, on a lightly floured surface roll dough into a 12x10-inch (30x25.5cm) rectangle 1/16 to ⅛ inch (1.5 to 3mm) thick. (*Or,* if using a pasta machine, pass dough through until 1/16 to ⅛ inch [1.5 to 3mm] thick.) Cut into sixteen 10x¾-inch (25.5x2cm) strips (see tip, page 57).

Cook pasta in boiling salted water until *almost* al dente (see photo 1, page 56). Allow 8 to 9 minutes for packaged mafaldine or 1 to 1½ minutes for Corn Pasta. Immediately drain. Rinse with cold water; drain well.

Arrange 8 strips of mafaldine in a greased 10x6x2-inch (25.5x6x5cm) baking dish. Trim to fit. Spoon *half* of the sauce over top (*see photo 3, page 57*). Sprinkle with *2 ounces (50g)* of the cheddar cheese. Repeat layers of noodles and sauce; reserve remaining cheese. Bake, covered, in a 350°F (180°C) gas mark 4 oven for 25 minutes. Uncover. Sprinkle remaining cheese on top (see photo 4, page 57). Bake 5 to 10 minutes more or until heated through. Let stand for 10 minutes before serving. Top with lettuce, crisps, olives, and tomato. Makes 6 main-dish servings.

Quick-Fixin' Lasagne

Here's your chance to be a magician. Put the lasagne strips into the dish uncooked, and watch them come out of the oven tender and scrumptious.

½ **pint (275ml) condensed cream of celery soup**
10 **ounces (275g) frozen broccoli spears, thawed and chopped**
2 **fluid ounces (55ml) dry white wine**
½ **teaspoon dried dill**
6 **packaged lasagne strips**
6 **ounces (175g) grated Swiss cheese**
8 **ounces (225g) chopped cooked chicken**
6 **fluid ounces (165ml) boiling water**

For sauce, in a medium mixing bowl stir together soup, broccoli, wine, and dill. Set aside.

Arrange 3 *uncooked* lasagne strips in a greased 10x6x2-inch (25.5x15x5cm) baking dish. Break to fit. Sprinkle with *half* of the cheese. Top with *half* of the chicken. Spoon *half* of the sauce over top (see photo 3, page 57). Repeat layers of pasta, cheese, chicken, and sauce. Pour water into the dish around the edges. Cover tightly with foil. Bake in a 350°F (180°C) gas mark 4 oven for 65 to 70 minutes or until pasta is tender. Let stand, covered, for 10 minutes. Makes 6 main-dish servings.

Spaetzle Specials

Pasta is a universal favourite, taking on different guises in nearly every cuisine. Here we have the German-created spaetzle (SHPETS luh).

   These small, irregularly shaped drops of batter are a cross between a noodle and a dumpling. As such, they're quite versatile. Small pasta shells can be substituted for spaetzle. Serve them in soup, use them under sauces, or try them as they're traditionally served in Germany—with sauerbraten.

Sausage-Spaetzle Vegetable Soup

Sausage-Spaetzle Vegetable Soup

¾ pound (350g) turkey and
    pork sausages
3 ounces (75g) sliced celery
4 ounces (110g) chopped onion
2 small cloves garlic, minced
2¼ pints (1.3l) water
2 ounces (50g) sliced carrots
1 tablespoon instant beef bouillon
    granules
2 bay leaves
1 teaspoon paprika
5 ounces (150g) plain flour
½ teaspoon salt
1 beaten egg
4 fluid ounces (110ml) milk
2 ounces (50g) grated cheddar cheese

In a large saucepan casserole cook sausages, celery, onion, and garlic until sausage is brown and vegetables are tender. Drain well.

Add water, carrots, beef bouillon granules, bay leaves, and paprika. Bring to boiling. Reduce heat, then simmer, covered, for 10 minutes. Remove bay leaves.

Meanwhile, for spaetzle batter, in a medium mixing bowl stir together flour and salt. Make a well in the centre of the mixture. In a small mixing bowl combine egg and milk. Add to flour mixture and mix well.

Return soup to boiling. Pour batter into a spaetzle maker or a colander with large holes (see photos 1–2). Hold the spaetzle maker or colander over boiling soup and press batter through (see photo 3). Simmer, uncovered, for 5 to 10 minutes or until spaetzle is al dente (see photo 2, page 14). Remove from heat immediately. Sprinkle with cheddar cheese. Makes 4 main-dish servings.

1 If you don't have a spaetzle maker, a colander with large holes will do. Measure the holes in the colander. They should be at least $3/16$ inch (4.5mm) in diameter for the batter to successfully flow through.

2 Set the spaetzle maker or colander on a piece of grease-proof paper. Pour the batter into the spaetzle maker or colander. You'll need to move quickly to the next step so the batter doesn't leak through.

3 Press the batter through the holes in the spaetzle maker. (Or, use a wooden spoon to press the batter through the colander holes, as shown.) The batter will fall into the boiling liquid in irregularly shaped droplets.

Sauerbraten-Style Swiss Steak

1	**pound (450g) rump steak, cut ¾ inch (2cm) thick**
4	**teaspoons plain flour**
2	**tablespoons cooking oil**
12	**fluid ounces (330ml) apple juice**
8	**ounces (225g) tinned sieved tomatoes**
2	**tablespoons vinegar**
1	**teaspoon prepared mustard**
6	**gingernuts, crushed**
10	**ounces (275g) plain flour**
2	**beaten eggs**
8	**fluid ounces (220ml) milk**

Cut beef into 4 serving-size pieces. Combine 4 teaspoons flour and ¼ teaspoon *salt*. Pound mixture into beef. In a 10-inch (25.5cm) frying pan cook beef in hot oil for 5 minutes, turning to brown evenly. Drain off fat.

In a small mixing bowl combine apple juice, sieved tomatoes, vinegar, mustard, and a dash of *pepper*. Pour over meat in frying pan. Bring to boiling. Reduce heat, then simmer, covered, over low heat about 1½ hours or until the meat is tender.

Remove meat from frying pan and cover. Stir gingernuts into tomato mixture in frying pan. Cook and stir until thickened and bubbly. Return meat to mixture; heat through.

Meanwhile, for spaetzle batter, in a large mixing bowl stir together 10 ounces (275g) flour and 1 teaspoon *salt*. Make a well in the centre of the mixture. In a small mixing bowl combine eggs and milk. Add to flour mixture and mix well.

In saucepan or casserole bring 5 pints (2.75l) *water* and 1 teaspoon *salt* to the boil. Pour batter into spaetzle maker or colander with large holes (see photos 1–2). Hold spaetzle maker or colander over saucepan; press batter through (see photo 3). Simmer, uncovered, until al dente (see photo 2, page 14). Immediately drain. Transfer to warm serving dish. Arrange meat mixture atop spaetzle. Makes 4 servings.

Basic Pasta Ribbons

Roll up your sleeves, put on an apron, and get ready for fun. It's time to make homemade pasta.

Making pasta from scratch is surprisingly easy. And the delicious results are worth the effort. If it's your first time, start with basic egg pasta. Then graduate to adding whole grain flour or a special seasoning to create a pasta that's an eating adventure.

Egg Pasta

Egg Pasta

12 ounces (350g) plain flour
½ teaspoon salt
2 beaten eggs
3 fluid ounces (75ml) water
1 teaspoon olive oil *or* cooking oil
Sliced cherry tomatoes (optional)
Snipped parsley (optional)

In a large mixing bowl stir together *10 ounces (275g)* of the flour and salt. Make a well in the centre of the mixture (see photo 1, page 76).

In a small mixing bowl combine eggs, water, and olive oil or cooking oil. Add to flour mixture and mix well (see photo 2, page 76).

Sprinkle the kneading surface with remaining flour. Turn dough out onto the floured surface. Knead until dough is smooth and elastic, 8 to 10 minutes (see photo 1). Cover and let rest for 10 minutes (see photo 2).

Divide dough into thirds or quarters. On a lightly floured surface roll each third of dough into a ¹/₁₆-inch-thick (1.5mm) rectangle about 16x12 inches (40x30cm), or each quarter of dough into a ¹/₁₆-inch-thick (1.5mm) square about 12x12 inches (30x30cm) (see photo 3). Cut as desired or as directed in recipe (see photo 4). (*Or,* if using a pasta machine, pass dough through until ¹/₁₆ inch [1.5mm] thick. Cut as desired [see tip, opposite].) Cook as directed on pages 120–121. If desired, garnish with cherry tomatoes and parsley. Makes 1 pound (450g) fresh pasta.

1 Sprinkle the kneading surface with the remaining flour and turn the dough out onto the floured surface. To knead, curve your fingers over the edge of the dough and pull it toward you. Then push down and away with the heel of your hand. Give the dough a quarter-turn, fold it toward you, and repeat the process. Keep kneading until the dough is smooth and elastic. For most pasta doughs, this will take 8 to 10 minutes.

2 Shape the dough into a ball and cover it with a towel to prevent it from drying. Let it rest for 10 minutes. This lets the dough relax and makes it easier to roll out.

3 To roll out the dough by hand, divide it into thirds or quarters. On a lightly floured surface, use a rolling pin to roll the dough to 1/16-inch (1.5mm) thickness. From a third of the dough, this will make a rectangle of about 16x12 inches (40x30cm). From a quarter of the dough, it will make a square of about 12x12 inches (30x30cm). The thickness of the dough is most important. So be sure, no matter how large your dough recipe is, that you end up with a rectangle or square 1/16 inch (1.5mm) thick.

4 Let the rolled-out dough stand 20 minutes so the surface dries slightly. Then roll up the dough loosely.

Linguine: Using a sharp knife, cut the dough into 1/8-inch-wide (3mm) slices.

Fettuccine or noodles: Cut the dough into 1/4-inch-wide (.5cm) slices.

Tagliatelle: Cut the dough into 1/2-inch-wide (1cm) slices.

Lift and shake to separate the strands. Cut noodles into 2-inch (5cm) lengths.

Using a Pasta Machine

Top: To roll out dough, set machine on widest opening and pass dough through. Reset on a narrower setting and pass dough through again. Repeat until dough is 1/16 inch (1.5mm) thick. As needed, dust dough with flour to prevent sticking.

Bottom: Pass dough through one of the machine's cutting blades, as shown.

Linguine: Use a 1/8-inch-wide (3mm) blade.

Fettuccine or noodles: Use a 1/4-inch-wide (.5cm) blade.

Tagliatelle: Use a 1/2-inch-wide (1cm) blade.

Cut noodles into 2-inch (5cm) lengths and other pastas into 12-inch (30cm) lengths.

Corn Pasta

7   ounces (200g) plain flour
5   ounces (150g) tortilla flour
        or cornmeal
2   beaten eggs
1   teaspoon olive oil *or* cooking oil

In a large mixing bowl stir together *5 ounces (150g)* of the plain flour, tortilla flour, and ½ teaspoon *salt.* Make a well in the centre of the mixture (see photo 1, page 76).

In a small bowl combine eggs, olive oil or cooking oil, and 3 fluid ounces (75ml) *water.* Add to flour mixture; mix well (see photo 2, page 76).

Sprinkle kneading surface with remaining plain flour. Turn dough onto floured surface. Knead until dough is smooth and elastic, 8 to 10 minutes (see photo 1, page 68). Cover and let rest 10 minutes (see photo 2, page 68).

Divide dough into thirds or quarters. On a lightly floured surface roll each third of dough into a ¹⁄₁₆-inch-thick (1.5mm) rectangle about 16x12 inches (40x30cm), or each quarter of dough into a ¹⁄₁₆-inch-thick (1.5mm) square about 12x12 inches (30x30cm) (see photo 3, page 69). Cut as desired (see photo 4, page 69). (*Or,* if using a pasta machine, pass dough through until ¹⁄₁₆ inch [1.5mm] thick. Cut as desired [see tip, page 69].) Cook as directed on pages 120–121. Makes 1 pound (450g) fresh pasta.

Pasta Diable

12   ounces (350g) plain flour
1   tablespoon chilli powder
2   beaten eggs
3   fluid ounces (75ml) water
1   teaspoon olive oil *or* cooking oil

In a mixing bowl stir together *10 ounces (275g)* of flour, chilli powder, and ½ teaspoon *salt.* Make a well in centre (see photo 1, page 76).

In a small mixing bowl combine eggs, water, and oil. Add to flour mixture and mix well (see photo 2, page 76).

Sprinkle the kneading surface with remaining flour. Turn dough out onto the floured surface. Knead until dough is smooth and elastic, 8 to 10 minutes (see photo 1, page 68). Cover and let rest 10 minutes (see photo 2, page 68).

Divide dough into thirds or quarters. On a lightly floured surface roll each third of dough into a ¹⁄₁₆-inch-thick (1.5mm) rectangle about 16x12 inches (40x30cm), or each quarter of dough into a ¹⁄₁₆-inch-thick (1.5mm) square about 12x12 inches (30x30cm) (see photo 3, page 69). Cut as desired or as directed in recipe (see photo 4, page 69). (*Or,* if using a pasta machine, pass dough through until ¹⁄₁₆ inch [1.5mm] thick. Cut as desired [see tip, page 69].) Cook as directed on pages 120–121. Makes 1 pound (450g) fresh pasta.

Making Pasta Dough in A Food Processor

You can whip up a batch of pasta dough in seconds if you have a food processor because it will do the kneading for you. Place the steel blade in the food processor bowl. Add *all* the dry ingredients and eggs. Cover and process until the mixture is the consistency of cornmeal. With the processor running, slowly pour the liquid ingredients through the feed tube. Continue processing *just* until the dough forms a ball. Let the dough rest; continue as recipe directs (see photos 2-4, pages 68-69).

Herb Pasta

Try making this pasta with one of the herbs we've listed here; next time experiment by adding your own choice.

12 **ounces (350g) plain flour**
 1 **teaspoon dried basil, marjoram, *or* sage, crushed**
½ **teaspoon salt**
 2 **beaten eggs**
 3 **fluid ounces (75ml) water**
 1 **teaspoon olive oil *or* cooking oil**

In a large mixing bowl stir together *10 ounces (275g)* of the flour; basil, marjoram, or sage; and salt. Make a well in the centre (see photo 1, page 76).

In a small mixing bowl combine eggs, water, and olive oil or cooking oil. Add to flour mixture and mix well (see photo 2, page 76).

Sprinkle the kneading surface with remaining flour. Turn dough out onto the floured surface. Knead until dough is smooth and elastic, 8 to 10 minutes (see photo 1, page 68). Cover and let rest 10 minutes (see photo 2, page 68).

Divide dough into thirds or quarters. On a lightly floured surface roll each third of dough into a ¹/₁₆-inch-thick (1.5mm) rectangle about 16x12 inches (40x30cm), or each quarter of dough into a ¹/₁₆-inch-thick (1.5mm) square about 12x12 inches (30x30cm) (see photo 3, page 69). Cut as desired or as directed in recipe (see photo 4, page 69). (*Or,* if using a pasta machine, pass dough through until ¹/₁₆ inch [1.5mm] thick. Cut as desired [see tip, page 69].) Cook as directed on pages 120–121. Makes 1 pound (450g) fresh pasta.

Whole Grain Pasta

Enjoy the toasty wheat flavour and whole grain texture that wheat germ adds to this pasta.

10 **ounces (275g) whole wheat flour**
 4 **tablespoons toasted wheat germ**
½ **teaspoon salt**
 2 **beaten eggs**
 3 **fluid ounces (75ml) water**
 1 **teaspoon olive oil *or* cooking oil**

In a large mixing bowl stir together *8 ounces (225g)* of the flour, wheat germ, and salt. Make a well in the centre of the mixture (see photo 1, page 76).

In a small mixing bowl combine eggs, water, and olive oil or cooking oil. Add to flour mixture and mix well (see photo 2, page 76).

Sprinkle the kneading surface with remaining flour. Turn dough out onto the floured surface. Knead until dough is smooth and elastic, 8 to 10 minutes (see photo 1, page 68). Cover and let rest 10 minutes (see photo 2, page 68).

Divide dough into thirds or quarters. On a lightly floured surface roll each third of dough into a ¹/₁₆-inch-thick (1.5mm) rectangle about 16x12 inches (40x30cm), or each quarter of dough into a ¹/₁₆-inch-thick (1.5mm) square about 12x12 inches (30x30cm) (see photo 3, page 69). Cut as desired or as directed in recipe (see photo 4, page 69). (*Or,* if using a pasta machine, pass dough through until ¹/₁₆ inch [1.5mm] thick. Cut as desired [see tip, page 69].) Cook as directed on pages 120–121. Makes 1 pound (450g) fresh pasta.

Whole Wheat Pasta: Prepare Whole Grain Pasta as above, *except* use 12 ounces (350g) *whole wheat flour* and omit the toasted wheat germ. In a large mixing bowl stir together *10 ounces (275g)* of the flour and salt. Make a well in the centre of the mixture (see photo 1, page 76). Continue as directed above.

Garlic Pasta

Toss some cooked Garlic Pasta with butter and Parmesan cheese for an outstanding side dish.

12 ounces (350g) plain flour
1 tablespoon onion powder
2 teaspoons garlic powder
½ teaspoon salt
2 beaten eggs
3 fluid ounces (80ml) water
1 teaspoon olive oil *or* cooking oil

In a large mixing bowl stir together *10 ounces (275g)* of the flour, onion powder, garlic powder, and salt. Make a well in the centre of the mixture (see photo 1, page 76).

In a small mixing bowl combine eggs, water, and olive oil or cooking oil. Add to flour mixture and mix well (see photo 2, page 76).

Sprinkle the kneading surface with remaining flour. Turn dough out onto the floured surface. Knead until dough is smooth and elastic, 8 to 10 minutes (see photo 1, page 68). Cover and let rest 10 minutes (see photo 2, page 68).

Divide dough into thirds or quarters. On a lightly floured surface roll each third of dough into a ¹⁄16-inch-thick (1.5mm) rectangle about 16x12 inches (40x30cm), or each quarter of dough into a ¹⁄16-inch-thick (1.5mm) square about 12x12 inches (30x30cm) (see photo 3, page 69). Cut as desired or as directed in recipe (see photo 4, page 69). (*Or,* if using a pasta machine, pass dough through until ¹⁄16 inch [1.5mm] thick. Cut as desired [see tip, page 69].) Cook as directed on pages 120–121. Makes 1 pound (450g) fresh pasta.

Oat Pasta

Use this mild-flavoured pasta as you would an egg pasta.

3 ounces (75g) rolled oats
9 ounces (250g) plain flour
½ teaspoon salt
2 beaten eggs
3 fluid ounces (80ml) water
1 teaspoon olive oil *or* cooking oil

Place oats in a food processor bowl or blender container. Cover, then process or blend until finely ground. In a large mixing bowl stir ground oats, *7 ounces (200g)* of the flour, and salt. Make a well in centre (see photo 1, page 76).

In a small mixing bowl combine eggs, water, and olive oil or cooking oil. Add to flour mixture and mix well (see photo 2, page 76).

Sprinkle the kneading surface with remaining flour. Turn dough out onto the floured surface. Knead until dough is smooth and elastic, 8 to 10 minutes (see photo 1, page 68). Cover and let rest 10 minutes (see photo 2, page 68).

Divide dough into thirds or quarters. On a lightly floured surface roll each third of dough into a ¹⁄16-inch-thick (1.5mm) rectangle about 16x12 inches (40x30cm), or each quarter of dough into a ¹⁄16-inch-thick (1.5mm) square about 12x12 inches (30x30cm) (see photo 3, page 69). Cut as desired or as directed in recipe (see photo 4, page 69). (*Or,* if using a pasta machine, pass dough through until ¹⁄16 inch [1.5mm] thick. Cut as desired [see tip, page 69].) Cook as directed on pages 120–121. Makes 1 pound (450g) fresh pasta.

Parsley Pasta

11 ounces (300g) plain flour
6 ounces (175g) snipped parsley
½ teaspoon salt
2 beaten eggs
3 tablespoons water
1 teaspoon olive oil *or* cooking oil

In a large mixing bowl stir together *10 ounces (275g)* of the flour, parsley, and salt. Make a well in the centre of the mixture (see photo 1, page 76).

In a small mixing bowl combine eggs, water, and olive oil or cooking oil. Add to flour mixture and mix well (see photo 2, page 76).

Sprinkle the kneading surface with remaining flour. Turn dough out onto the floured surface. Knead until dough is smooth and elastic, 8 to 10 minutes (see photo 1, page 68). Cover and let rest 10 minutes (see photo 2, page 68).

Divide dough into thirds or quarters. On a lightly floured surface roll each third of dough into a ¹⁄₁₆-inch-thick (1.5mm) rectangle about 16x12 inches (40x30cm), or each quarter of dough into a ¹⁄₁₆-inch-thick (1.5mm) square about 12x12 inches (30x30cm) (see photo 3, page 69). Cut as desired or as directed in recipe (see photo 4, page 69). (*Or,* if using a pasta machine, pass dough through until ¹⁄₁₆ inch [1.5mm] thick. Cut as desired [see tip, page 69].) Cook as directed on pages 120–121. Makes 1 pound (450g) fresh pasta.

Storing Homemade Pasta

When you aren't going to use your pasta right after cutting or shaping it, you'll want to let it dry and then store it in the refrigerator or freezer.

For unstuffed pasta, start by spreading it out on a pasta drying rack. Or, improvise your own drying rack by draping the pasta over a wire cooling rack or by hanging it over a clothes hanger. If you plan to use the pasta within a few days, let it dry overnight or until it is completely dry. Then wrap it in clingfilm or foil, or place it in an airtight container. Store the pasta in the refrigerator for up to 3 days.

You may also freeze unstuffed pasta. Before freezing, spread it out to dry for at least 1 hour. Then seal it in moisture- and vapourproof wrap. You can freeze it up to 8 months.

For stuffed pasta, start by dusting it lightly with flour and letting it dry for 1 hour. If you plan to use it within a day or two, put it in a covered container in the refrigerator. To keep it longer, however, place the pasta on a baking sheet, cover, and freeze until firm. Then seal it in moisture- and vapourproof wrap and freeze it up to 8 months.

Gourmet Pasta Shapes

Now that you're an expert at making basic pasta, try some of these easy embellishments. First, add nuts, a vegetable, or fruit juice to create a pasta with gourmet flair. Then form special shapes such as bow ties or mushroom caps. Top it all with your favourite sauce, and you've got a meal *extraordinaire.*

Pasta Verde

Pasta Verde

Whole wheat flour gives this green (verde) pasta a coarse texture.

10 ounces (275g) frozen chopped
     spinach or broccoli
 2 eggs
 1 teaspoon olive oil *or* cooking oil
12 ounces (350g) plain flour
 5 ounces (150g) whole wheat flour
½ teaspoon salt

Cook spinach or broccoli according to package directions. Drain well in a colander, using a spoon to press out as much liquid as possible.

In a blender container or a food processor bowl combine cooked spinach or broccoli, eggs, and olive oil or cooking oil. Cover, then blend or process until smooth.

In a large mixing bowl stir together *10 ounces (275g)* of the plain flour, whole wheat flour, and salt. Make a well in the centre (see photo 1). Add spinach mixture and mix until thoroughly blended (see photo 2).

Sprinkle kneading surface with remaining flour. Turn dough onto floured surface. Knead until dough is smooth and elastic, 8 to 10 minutes (see photo 1, page 68). Cover and let rest 10 minutes (see photo 2, page 68).

Divide dough into thirds or quarters. Roll, cut, or shape as desired or as directed in recipe (see tips, opposite). Cook as directed on pages 120–121. If desired, garnish with carrot curls and parsley. Makes 1½ pounds (700g) fresh pasta.

1 In a large mixing bowl stir together the dry ingredients. Then use a wooden spoon to push the flour mixture against the edge of the bowl, making a well in the centre.

2 Combine the liquid ingredients. Then pour the mixture all at once into the well in the centre of the dry ingredients. Mix with a wooden spoon, as shown, until all ingredients are well combined.

Making Farfalle

To make farfalle (bow ties), roll out a third or quarter of the dough to $1/16$-inch (1.5mm) thickness (see photo 3, page 69). Using a fluted pastry wheel or a sharp knife, cut the dough into rectangles that are 2 inches (5cm) long and 1 inch (2.5cm) wide.

To form the bow tie shape, pinch the centre of each rectangle, as shown. Gather and cover any scraps of dough so they can be rerolled. Repeat with the remaining dough.

Making Tripolini

To make tripolini, roll out a third or quarter of the dough to $1/16$-inch (1.5mm) thickness (see photo 3, page 69). Using a 1-inch-round (2.5cm) cutter, cut the dough into circles. Pinch the centre of each circle, forming a rounded butterfly shape. Gather and cover any dough scraps so they can be rerolled. Repeat with the remaining dough.

Making Mushroom Caps

Shape a quarter of the dough into a roll $\frac{1}{2}$ inch (1cm) in diameter. Cover remaining dough. Cut roll into $\frac{1}{8}$-inch-thick (3mm) slices. Place 1 slice in your palm. Press the middle with your index finger, making an indentation. (Or, use a wooden spoon handle.) Twist your finger to broaden the cap. Flour hands as needed. Repeat.

Orange Pasta

Choose from this rainbow of fruit flavours for a scrumptious change-of-pace pasta.

1 pound (450g) plain flour
½ teaspoon finely grated orange peel
2 beaten eggs
6 fluid ounces (165ml) orange juice
    concentrate
1 teaspoon olive oil *or* cooking oil

In a mixing bowl stir together *15 ounces (425g)* of the flour and orange peel. Make a well in the centre of the mixture (see photo 1, page 76).

In a small bowl combine eggs, juice concentrate, and olive oil or cooking oil. Add to flour mixture and mix well (see photo 2, page 76).

Sprinkle the kneading surface with remaining flour. Turn dough out onto the floured surface. Knead until dough is smooth and elastic, 8 to 10 minutes (see photo 1, page 68). Cover and let rest 10 minutes (see photo 2, page 68).

Divide dough into thirds or quarters. Roll, cut, or shape as desired or as directed in recipe (see tips, page 77). Cook as directed on pages 120–121. Makes 1½ pounds (700g) fresh pasta.

Lemon Pasta: Prepare Orange Pasta as above, *except* omit orange peel; add ½ teaspoon *salt* to the flour; and substitute 6 fluid ounces (165ml) *concentrated lemonade* for the orange juice concentrate.

Apple Pasta: Prepare Orange Pasta as above, *except* omit orange peel; add ½ teaspoon *salt* to the flour; and substitute 6 fluid ounces (165ml) *apple juice concentrate* for the orange juice concentrate.

Carrot Pasta

Brightly coloured vegetable pasta!

1 pound (450g) tinned carrots, diced
    and well drained
2 eggs
1 pound 2 ounces (500g) plain flour
½ teaspoon salt
1 teaspoon olive oil *or* cooking oil

In a blender container or a food processor bowl, combine carrots and eggs. Cover, then blend or process until smooth.

In a large mixing bowl stir together *1 pound (450g)* of the flour and salt. Make a well in the centre of the mixture (see photo 1, page 76). Add carrot mixture and olive oil or cooking oil; mix well (see photo 2, page 76).

Sprinkle the kneading surface with remaining flour. Turn dough out onto the floured surface. Knead until dough is smooth and elastic, 8 to 10 minutes (see photo 1, page 68). Cover and let rest 10 minutes (see photo 2, page 68).

Divide dough into third or quarters. Roll, cut, or shape as desired or as directed in recipe (see tips, page 77). Cook as directed on pages 120–121. Makes 1¾ pounds (810g) fresh pasta.

Beetroot Pasta: Prepare Carrot Pasta as above, *except* substitute 1 pound (450g) tinned sliced beetroot, well drained, for the carrots.

Nut Pasta

5 ounces (150g) slivered almonds, toasted
12 ounces (350g) plain flour
½ teaspoon salt
2 beaten eggs
3 fluid ounces (80ml) water
1 teaspoon walnut oil, hazelnut oil, *or* cooking oil

In a food processor bowl or a blender container place almonds. Cover; process or blend until almonds are very finely chopped. In a large mixing bowl stir together almonds, *10 ounces (275g)* of the flour, and salt. Make a well in the centre of the mixture (see photo 1, page 76).

In a small mixing bowl combine eggs, water, and oil. Add to flour mixture and mix well (see photo 2, page 76).

Sprinkle the kneading surface with remaining flour. Turn dough out onto the floured surface. Knead until dough is smooth and elastic, 8 to 10 minutes (see photo 1, page 68). Cover and let rest 10 minutes (see photo 2, page 68).

Divide dough into thirds or quarters. Roll, cut, or shape as desired or as directed in recipe (see tips, page 77). Cook as directed on pages 120–121. Makes 1¼ pounds (560g) fresh pasta.

Tomato-Herb Pasta

1 pound 2 ounces (500g) plain flour
1 teaspoon dried basil or oregano, crushed
½ teaspoon salt
2 beaten eggs
8 ounces (225g) tinned sieved tomatoes
1 teaspoon olive oil *or* cooking oil

In a large bowl stir together *1 pound (450g)* of the flour, basil or oregano, and salt. Make a well in the centre (see photo 1, page 76).

In a small bowl combine eggs, sieved tomatoes, and olive oil or cooking oil. Add to flour mixture and mix well (see photo 2, page 76).

Sprinkle the kneading surface with remaining flour. Turn dough out onto the floured surface. Knead until dough is smooth and elastic, 8 to 10 minutes (see photo 1, page 68). Cover and let rest 10 minutes (see photo 2, page 68).

Divide dough into thirds or quarters. Roll, cut, or shape as desired or as directed in recipe (see tips, page 77). Cook as directed on pages 120–121. Makes 1½ pounds (700g) fresh pasta.

A Pasta Machine Helps Knead Dough

A pasta machine can ease the task of kneading dough. After mixing the dough, start kneading it by hand *just* until you work in the remaining flour. The dough *won't* be smooth and elastic yet. Divide the dough into thirds or quarters and coat with more flour. With the pasta machine on the widest setting, feed through one portion of the dough. (Keep remaining dough covered.) Fold the dough in half, coat with more flour, and run it through the same setting. Repeat this until the dough is smooth and no longer tears. Repeat with remaining dough.

Manicotti And Cannelloni

It's all in the way you roll it. Roll a rectangle of pasta diagonally and you've created manicotti. Roll it straight and you have cannelloni.

Of course, one thing remains the same; both of these homemade pasta tubes brim with enticing fillings. So, whichever you choose, you'll enjoy a marvellous dish of pasta.

Crab Manicotti

Crab Manicotti

1	**ounce (25 g) butter *or* margarine**
1	**ounce (25g) plain flour**
12	**fluid ounces (330ml) single cream *or* milk**
2	**ounces (50g) grated Swiss cheese**
12	**ounces (350g) frozen crabmeat thawed, drained, and flaked, *or* tinned crabmeat, drained**
10	**ounces (275g) frozen broccoli thawed, drained, and chopped**
⅛	**teaspoon dried dill**
⅓	**recipe Egg Pasta (see page 68) *or* 8 packaged manicotti *or* cannelloni shells**

For sauce, in a medium saucepan melt butter or margarine. Stir in flour. Add single cream or milk all at once. Cook and stir until thickened and bubbly. Stir in cheese until melted.

For filling, stir together *4 fluid ounces (110ml)* of the sauce, crabmeat, broccoli, and dill.

If using Egg Pasta, roll dough into a 14x10-inch (35x25.5cm) rectangle ¹⁄₁₆ to ⅛ inch (1.5 to 3mm) thick. Cut dough into eight 5x3½-inch (13x8.5cm) rectangles (see photo 1).

Cook pasta in boiling salted water until al dente (see photos 1–2, page 14). Allow 2 to 3 minutes for Egg Pasta manicotti or 18 minutes for packaged manicotti. Drain. Rinse with cold water, then drain well (see photo 1, page 20).

For Egg Pasta manicotti, place 1 rectangle with 1 corner toward you. Spoon about *3 tablespoons* filling diagonally across rectangle, then roll pasta around filling (see photo 2). Repeat. *Or,* for packaged manicotti, spoon *3 tablespoons* filling into *each* shell (see tip, opposite).

Arrange filled manicotti in a 12x7½x2-inch (30x19x5cm) baking dish (see photo 3). Pour remaining sauce over top. Sprinkle with paprika, if desired. Cover with foil. Bake in a 350°F (180°C) gas mark 4 oven for 25 to 30 minutes or until heated through. If desired, garnish with tomato roses and sprigs of fresh herb. Makes 4 main-dish servings.

1 To make homemade manicotti shells, roll the pasta dough into a 14x10-inch (36x25.5cm) rectangle that is between ¹⁄₁₆ and ⅛ inch (1.5 and 3mm) thick. Use a sharp knife to cut the dough into eight 5x3½-inch (13x8.5cm) rectangles.

2 To fill manicotti, place the cooked pasta rectangle with 1 corner toward you. Spoon about 5 tablespoons of the filling diagonally across and just below the centre of the rectangle. Then, beginning at the bottom corner of the rectangle, roll the dough diagonally around the filling, as shown.

3 Carefully transfer the filled manicotti shells to a 12x7½x2-inch (30x19x5cm) baking dish. Place them in the dish with the corners or seams on the bottom so they don't come unrolled.

Stuffing Packaged Manicotti Shells

If you're using packaged manicotti shells, you'll find that they're already rolled into tubes. To fill them, use a small spoon and stuff about 5 tablespoons of the filling into each cooked shell. Use a spoon that is smaller in diameter than the shell so you can reach the centre without tearing the pasta.

Saucy Italian Manicotti

1	pound (450g) spicy sausage meat
4	ounces (110g) chopped carrot
4	ounces (110g) chopped onion
1	clove garlic, minced
28	ounces (780g) tinned tomatoes
6	ounces (175g) tomato puree
2	teaspoons Italian seasoning
⅓	recipe Garlic Pasta (see page 72) or 8 packaged manicotti shells
4	ounces (110g) grated mozzarella cheese

In a 10-inch (25.5cm) frying pan cook sausage meat, carrot, onion, and garlic until meat is brown and vegetables are tender. Drain off fat. Drain tomatoes, reserving 8 fluid ounces (225ml) juice. Chop tomatoes. Add tomatoes, tomato puree, and seasoning to sausage. Bring to boiling; lower heat to medium-low. Cook, uncovered, for 10 minutes, stirring occasionally.

Meanwhile, if using Garlic Pasta, roll dough into a 14x10-inch (35x25.5cm) rectangle ¹⁄₁₆ to ⅛ inch (1.5 to 3mm) thick. Cut dough into eight 5x3½-inch (13x8.5cm) rectangles (see photo 1, page 82).

Cook pasta in boiling salted water until al dente (see photos 1–2, page 14). Allow 2 to 3 minutes for Garlic Pasta manicotti or 18 minutes for packaged manicotti. Drain. Rinse with cold water, then drain well (see photo 1, page 20).

For Garlic Pasta manicotti, place 1 rectangle with 1 corner toward you. Spoon *3 tablespoons* filling diagonally across rectangle, then roll pasta around filling (see photo 2, page 82). Repeat. (*Or,* for packaged manicotti, spoon *3 tablespoons* filling into *each* shell [see tip, page 83].)

Arrange filled manicotti in a 12x7½x2-inch (30x19x5cm) baking dish (see photo 3, page 82). Stir reserved tomato juice into remaining filling. Pour over manicotti. Cover with foil. Bake in a 350°F (180°C) gas mark 4 oven for 30 to 35 minutes or until heated through. Remove foil and sprinkle with cheese. Bake for 2 to 3 minutes more or until cheese is melted. Makes 4 main-dish servings.

Beef and Cheese Manicotti

¾	pound (350g) minced beef
4	ounces (110g) chopped onion
2	small cloves garlic, minced
8	ounces (225g) cottage cheese, drained
1	ounce (25g) grated Parmesan cheese
1	beaten egg
2	tablespoons snipped parsley
⅓	recipe Pasta Diable (see page 70) *or* 8 packaged manicotti *or* cannelloni shells
15	ounces (425g) tinned sieved tomatoes
2	ounces (50g) grated cheddar cheese
	Snipped parsley

For filling, in a 10-inch (25.5cm) frying pan cook beef, onion, and garlic until beef is brown and onion is tender. Drain off fat. Stir in cottage cheese, Parmesan cheese, egg, and 2 tablespoons snipped parsley. Set aside.

If using Pasta Diable, roll dough into a 14x10-inch (35x25.5cm) rectangle ¹⁄₁₆ to ⅛ inch (1.5 to 3mm) thick. Cut dough into eight 5x3½-inch (13x8.5cm) rectangles (see photo 1, page 82).

Cook pasta in boiling salted water until al dente (see photos 1–2, page 14). Allow 2 to 3 minutes for Pasta Diable manicotti or 18 minutes for packaged manicotti. Drain. Rinse with cold water, then drain well (see photo 1, page 20).

For Pasta Diable manicotti, place 1 rectangle with 1 corner toward you. Spoon about *3 tablespoons* of the filling diagonally across rectangle, then roll pasta around filling (see photo 2, page 82). Repeat with remaining rectangles. *Or,* for packaged manicotti, spoon about *3 tablespoons* of the filling into *each* shell (see tip, page 83).

Arrange filled manicotti in a 12x7½x2-inch (30x19x5cm) baking dish (see photo 3, page 82). Pour sieved tomatoes over top. Cover with foil. Bake in a 350°F (180°C) gas mark 4 oven about 35 minutes or until heated through. Sprinkle with cheddar cheese. Garnish with additional parsley. Makes 4 main-dish servings.

Ricotta and Ham Cannelloni

1	ounce (25g) butter *or* margarine
1	ounce (25g) plain flour
1/8	teaspoon salt
1/8	teaspoon ground nutmeg
1/8	teaspoon pepper
14	fluid ounces (385ml) milk
2	tablespoons snipped parsley
5	ounces (150g) frozen chopped spinach, thawed and well drained
4	ounces (110g) diced cooked ham
8	ounces (225g) ricotta cheese
1/2	teaspoon dried marjoram, crushed
1/4	recipe Pasta Verde (see page 76) *or* 8 packaged cannelloni shells
1	ounce (25g) grated Parmesan cheese

For sauce, in a medium saucepan melt butter or margarine. Stir in flour, salt, nutmeg, and pepper. Add milk all at once. Cook and stir until mixture is thickened and bubbly. Stir in snipped parsley. Set aside.

For filling, stir together spinach, ham, ricotta cheese, and marjoram. Stir in *2 fluid ounces (55ml)* of the sauce. Set aside.

If using Pasta Verde, roll the dough into a 14x10-inch (35x25.5cm) rectangle 1/16 to 1/8 inch (1.5 to 3mm) thick. Cut dough into eight 5x3½-inch (13x8.5cm) rectangles (see photo 1, page 82).

Cook pasta in boiling salted water until al dente (see photos 1–2, page 14). Allow 2 to 3 minutes for Pasta Verde cannelloni or 18 minutes for packaged cannelloni. Drain. Rinse with cold water, then drain well (see photo 1, page 20).

For Pasta Verde cannelloni, fill and roll rectangles as directed in the tip below. *Or,* for packaged cannelloni, spoon about *3 tablespoons* of the filling into *each* shell (see tip, page 85).

Arrange filled cannelloni in a 12x7½x2-inch (30x19x5cm) baking dish (see photo 3, page 82). Pour remaining sauce over top. Sprinkle with Parmesan cheese. Cover with foil. Bake in a 350°F (180°C) gas mark 4 oven for 25 to 30 minutes or until heated through. Makes 4 main-dish servings.

Filling Cannelloni

Cannelloni is the same size as manicotti. It's just rolled a little differently.

To fill cannelloni, place the cooked pasta rectangle with one of the long sides toward you. Spoon about *3 tablespoons* of the filling straight across and just below the centre of *each* rectangle. Then, beginning at the bottom edge of the rectangle, roll the dough around the filling, as shown.

Filled Pasta Dumplings

If variety is the spice of life, then pasta is well seasoned. It comes in what seems to be an endless supply of shapes and sizes, all of which can be used in an infinite variety of dishes, including salads and desserts.

In this chapter, pasta displays two more of its shapes—ravioli and filled stars. Each pasta pocket has a tasty filling tucked inside that will add flavour and visual variety to your pasta repertoire.

Basil Ravioli Salad

Basil Ravioli Salad

- **2 ounces (50g) finely chopped walnuts**
- **1 ounce (25g) finely chopped pine nuts *or* almonds**
- **3 ounces (75g) cream cheese with chives, softened**
- **2 tablespoons grated Parmesan cheese**
- **1 teaspoon snipped fresh basil *or* ¼ teaspoon dried basil, crushed**
- **⅔ recipe Egg Pasta (see page 68)**
- **1 courgette, halved lengthwise and thinly sliced**
- **3 fluid ounces (80ml) salad oil**
- **2 fluid ounces (55ml) dry white wine**
- **3 tablespoons lemon juice**
- **1 tablespoon caster sugar**
- **2 teaspoons snipped fresh basil *or* ¾ teaspoon dried basil, crushed**
- **½ teaspoon salt**
- **⅛ teaspoon pepper**
- **2 tomatoes, cut into thin wedges**

For filling, in a small mixing bowl stir together walnuts, pine nuts or almonds, cream cheese, Parmesan cheese, and 1 teaspoon fresh basil or ¼ teaspoon dried basil. Set aside.

On a lightly floured surface roll out pasta until ¹/₁₆ inch (1.5mm) thick. Cut into 2-inch-wide (5cm) strips. Place about *1 teaspoon* of the filling at 1-inch (2.5cm) intervals on 1 strip (see photo 1). Moisten pasta around filling. Lay another strip on top; seal and cut apart (see photo 2). Repeat.

(*Or,* to make ravioli using a ravioli frame, on a lightly floured surface roll out pasta until ¹/₁₆ inch [1.5mm] thick. Lightly flour the hollows of the frame. Place a sheet of pasta over the frame, fill, top with a second sheet of pasta, and cut into ravioli [see tip, opposite].)

Cook ravioli in boiling salted water until al dente (see photos 1–2, page 14). Allow 6 to 8 minutes. Immediately drain.

Cook courgette in a small amount of boiling water for 2 to 3 minutes. Drain. Cover and chill.

For dressing, in a screw-top jar combine oil, wine, lemon juice, sugar, 2 teaspoons fresh basil or ¾ teaspoon dried basil, salt, and pepper. Cover and shake to mix.

In a large bowl, combine ravioli and dressing. Toss to mix well. Cover and chill several hours or overnight, stirring occasionally. Before serving, add chilled courgette and tomatoes. Toss to mix. Makes 8 side-dish servings.

1 Use a sharp knife or fluted pastry wheel to cut the rolled dough into 2-inch-wide (5cm) strips for ravioli. Place the filling at 1-inch (2.5cm) intervals on the dough strip. Leave a ½-inch (1cm) margin around the edges.

2 Moisten the dough around the filling by brushing it with water. Lay a second strip of dough on top of the first. Then press down with the side of your hand to seal the two strips of dough around each mound of filling. To separate ravioli, cut halfway between the mounds of filling with a fluted pastry wheel or sharp knife.

Using a Ravioli Frame

Cut a piece of dough that is a little longer and wider than the frame. Place the sheet of dough over the frame, making sure the dough completely covers the frame. Use your fingers to lightly press the dough into the hollows of the frame. Then fill *each* hollow with about *1 teaspoon* of the filling.

Moisten the dough around the filling by brushing it with water. Top the filled dough with another sheet of pasta dough that completely covers the frame. Roll a standard rolling pin over the top, pressing firmly to seal and score the ravioli.

To remove the ravioli, carefully invert the frame onto a floured surface. (You may need to tap one end of the frame against the surface to dislodge the ravioli.) With a fluted pastry wheel or sharp knife, cut the dough into individual ravioli; trim excess dough. Repeat with remaining dough.

Mushroom-Filled Ravioli

A savoury filling with the texture of a mushroom pâté.

4 ounces (110g) very finely chopped mushrooms
3 ounces (75g) very finely chopped onion
1 clove garlic, minced
1 tablespoon butter *or* margarine
1 beaten egg
1 ounce (25g) fine dry seasoned breadcrumbs
1 ounce (25g) grated Parmesan cheese
¼ teaspoon dried thyme, crushed
¼ recipe Pasta Verde (see page 76)
8 fluid ounces (220ml) whipping cream
1 ounce (25g) sliced stoned ripe olives (optional)

For filling, in a 10-inch (25.5cm) frying pan cook mushrooms, onion, and garlic in hot butter or margarine until tender. Stir together mushroom mixture, egg, breadcrumbs, Parmesan cheese, and thyme. Set aside.

On a lightly floured surface roll out pasta until ¹/₁₆ inch (1.5mm) thick. Cut into 2-inch-wide (5cm) strips. Place about *1 teaspoon* of the filling at 1-inch (2.5cm) intervals on 1 strip (see photo 1, page 88). Moisten pasta around filling. Lay another strip on top; seal and cut apart (see photo 2, page 89). Repeat.

(*Or,* to make ravioli using a ravioli frame, on a lightly floured surface roll out pasta until ¹/₁₆ inch [1.5mm] thick. Lightly flour the hollows of the frame. Place a sheet of pasta over the frame, fill, top with a second sheet of pasta, and cut into ravioli [see tip, page 89]. Repeat.)

In a small saucepan cook cream over medium-low heat for 15 to 20 minutes or until thickened, stirring frequently.

Meanwhile, cook ravioli in boiling salted water until al dente (see photos 1–2, page 14). Allow 6 to 8 minutes. Immediately drain. Pour thickened cream over cooked ravioli. If desired, garnish with olives. Makes 6 side-dish servings.

Pizza Ravioli

Flavour-packed ravioli that mimic the taste of pizza.

1 beaten egg
2 ounces (50g) grated mozzarella cheese
3 ounces (75g) cottage cheese
2 ounces (50g) pepperoni, sliced and finely chopped
1 tablespoon fine dry breadcrumbs
½ recipe Egg Pasta (see page 68)
   Chunky Pizza Sauce
1 ounce (25g) grated mozzarella cheese

For filling, in a small mixing bowl stir together egg, 2 ounces (50g) mozzarella cheese, cottage cheese, pepperoni, and breadcrumbs. Set aside.

On a lightly floured surface roll out pasta until ¹/₁₆ inch (1.5mm) thick. Cut into 2-inch-wide (5cm) strips. Place about *1 teaspoon* of the filling at 1-inch (2.5cm) intervals on 1 strip (see photo 1, page 88). Moisten pasta around filling. Lay another strip on top; seal and cut apart (see photo 2, page 89). Repeat.

(*Or,* to make ravioli using a ravioli frame, on a lightly floured surface roll out pasta until ¹/₁₆ inch [1.5mm] thick. Lightly flour the hollows of the frame. Place a sheet of pasta over the frame, fill, top with a second sheet of pasta, and cut into ravioli [see tip, page 89]. Repeat.)

Prepare Chunky Pizza Sauce. Meanwhile, cook ravioli in boiling salted water until al dente (see photos 1–2, page 14). Allow 6 to 8 minutes. Immediately drain. Pour Chunky Pizza Sauce over cooked ravioli. Sprinkle with 1 ounce (25g) mozzarella cheese. Makes 5 main-dish servings.

Chunky Pizza Sauce: In a medium saucepan cook 2 ounces (50g) chopped *onion* and 2 ounces (50g) chopped *green pepper* in 1 ounce (25g) hot *butter or margarine* until tender but not brown. Stir in ¾ pint (425ml) tinned *sieved tomatoes;* 2 ounces (50g) tinned chopped *mushrooms,* drained; 1 teaspoon *Italian seasoning;* and ½ teaspoon *caster sugar.* Bring to boiling. Reduce heat; then simmer, covered, for 10 minutes.

Chocolate-Almond-Filled Ravioli With Cherry Sauce

Here's a deliciously elegant pasta dessert.

1 **beaten egg yolk**
3 **ounces (75g) cream cheese, softened**
1 **ounce (25g) icing sugar**
1 **drop vanilla essence**
1 **ounce (25g) finely chopped toasted almonds**
1 **ounce (25g) plain chocolate, grated**
½ **teaspoon finely grated orange peel**
⅓ **recipe Orange Pasta *or* Lemon Pasta (see page 78)**
1 **pound (450g) fresh *or* frozen unsweetened stoned tart red cherries**
3 **ounces (75g) caster sugar**
1 **tablespoon cornflour**

For filling, in a small mixing bowl beat together egg yolk, cream cheese, icing sugar, and vanilla. Stir in almonds, grated chocolate, and orange peel. Set aside.

On a lightly floured surface roll out pasta until ¹⁄₁₆ inch (1.5mm) thick. Cut into 2-inch-wide (5cm) strips. Place about *1 teaspoon* of the filling at 1-inch (2.5cm) intervals on 1 strip (see photo 1, page 88). Moisten pasta around filling. Lay another strip on top; seal and cut (see photo 2, page 89). Repeat.

(*Or,* to make ravioli using a ravioli frame, on a lightly floured surface roll out pasta until ¹⁄₁₆ inch [1.5mm] thick. Lightly flour the hollows of the frame. Place a sheet of pasta over the frame, fill, top with a second sheet of pasta, and cut into ravioli [see tip, page 89]. Repeat.)

For sauce, thaw cherries, if frozen. In a medium saucepan combine sugar and cornflour. Stir in 3 tablespoons *water*. Add cherries. Cook and stir until thickened and bubbly, then cook and stir 2 minutes more. Keep sauce warm.

Meanwhile, cook ravioli in boiling water until al dente (see photos 1–2, page 14). Allow 6 to 8 minutes. Immediately drain. Pour cherry sauce over cooked ravioli. Makes 8 dessert servings.

Turkey Soup

You may want to use a small ravioli frame to make this recipe. Smaller ravioli are easier to eat in soup.

2 **spring onions, sliced**
½ **teaspoon dried sage, crushed**
¼ **teaspoon salt**
⅛ **teaspoon pepper**
½ **pound (225g) minced raw turkey**
½ **recipe Whole Wheat Pasta (see page 71)**
2¾ **pints (1.55l) chicken stock**
3 **ounces (75g) sliced fresh mushrooms**
4 **ounces (110g) thinly sliced carrots**
4 **fluid ounces (110ml) water**
1 **ounce (25g) snipped parsley**
2 **spring onions, sliced**
2 **cloves garlic, minced**

For filling, in a medium mixing bowl combine 2 sliced spring onions, sage, salt, and pepper. Add turkey and mix well. Set aside.

On a lightly floured surface roll out pasta until ¹⁄₁₆ inch (1.5mm) thick. Cut into 2-inch-wide (5cm) strips. Place about *1 teaspoon* of the filling at 1-inch (2.5cm) intervals on 1 strip (see photo 1, page 88). Moisten pasta around filling. Lay another strip on top; seal and cut apart (see photo 2, page 89). Repeat.

(*Or,* to make ravioli using a ravioli frame, on a lightly floured surface roll out pasta until ¹⁄₁₆ inch [1.5mm] thick. Lightly flour the hollows of the frame. Place a sheet of pasta over the frame, fill, top with a second sheet of pasta, and cut into ravioli [see tip, page 89]. Repeat.)

In a large casserole combine chicken stock, mushrooms, carrots, water, parsley, 2 sliced spring onions, and garlic. Bring to boiling. Reduce heat, then simmer, covered, for 10 minutes. Uncover and return to boiling. Gradually add ravioli. Cook until pasta is al dente and filling is done (see photos 1–2, page 14). Allow 6 to 8 minutes more. Serves 8.

Ham and Cheese Stars

The colours in this dish echo those in the Italian flag—green pasta, white sauce, and a reddish ham filling.

1 **beaten egg**
½ **pound (225g) minced cooked ham**
8 **ounces (225g) ricotta cheese**
2 **ounces (50g) grated carrot**
½ **teaspoon dried basil, crushed**
½ **recipe Pasta Verde (see page 76)**
3 **ounces (75g) sliced fresh mushrooms**
4 **spring onions, sliced**
1 **ounce (25g) butter *or* margarine**
8 **fluid ounces (220ml) milk**
1 **tablespoon chopped pimento**
⅛ **teaspoon salt**
4 **ounces (110g) soured cream**
1 **ounce (25g) plain flour**

For filling, in a medium mixing bowl stir together egg, ham, cheese, carrot, and basil. Set aside.

On a lightly floured surface roll pasta into an 18-inch (45cm) square ¹/₁₆ (1.5mm) thick. Cut into 3-inch-wide (7.5cm) strips. Place about *1 tablespoon* of the filling on each strip at 2-inch (5cm) intervals (see photo 1, page 88). Cut pasta between mounds of filling, forming 3-inch (7.5cm) squares. Moisten pasta around filling. Form into stars (see tip, opposite).

Cook stars in boiling salted water until al dente (see photos 1–2, page 14). Allow 8 to 10 minutes. Immediately drain. Keep pasta warm.

Meanwhile, for sauce, in a medium saucepan cook mushrooms and spring onion in hot butter or margarine until tender. Stir in milk, pimento, and salt. In a small mixing bowl stir together soured cream and flour; gradually stir into milk mixture. Cook and stir until thickened and bubbly. Cook and stir 1 minute more. Pour over hot cooked stars. Makes 5 or 6 main-dish servings.

Spinach Ravioli in Herb-Tomato Sauce

5 **ounces (150g) frozen chopped spinach, thawed and well drained**
8 **ounces (225g) ricotta cheese**
½ **teaspoon dried marjoram, crushed**
¼ **teaspoon salt**
⅛ **teaspoon pepper**
⅔ **recipe Egg Pasta (see page 68)**
2 **ounces (50g) chopped onion**
1 **tablespoon butter *or* margerine**
15 **ounces (425g) tinned sieved tomatoes**
½ **teaspoon caster sugar**
½ **teaspoon dried oregano, crushed**
Grated Parmesan cheese (optional)

For filling, in a medium mixing bowl stir together spinach, ricotta cheese, marjoram, salt, and pepper. Set aside.

On a lightly floured surface roll out pasta until ¹/₁₆ inch (1.5mm) thick. Cut into 2-inch-wide (5cm) strips. Place about *1 teaspoon* of the filling at 1-inch (2.5cm) intervals on 1 strip (see photo 1, page 88). Moisten pasta around filling. Lay another strip on top; seal and cut apart (see photo 2, page 89). Repeat.

(*Or,* to make ravioli using a ravioli frame, on a lightly floured surface roll out pasta until ¹/₁₆ inch [1.5mm] thick. Lightly flour the hollows of the frame. Place a sheet of pasta over the frame, fill, top with a second sheet of pasta, and cut into ravioli [see tip, page 89]. Repeat.)

For herb-tomatoe sauce, cook onion in hot butter or margerine until tender. Stir in sieved tomatoes, caster sugar, and oregano. Bring to boiling. Reduce heat, then simmer, covered, for 5 minutes.

Cook *half* of the ravioli* in boiling salted water until al dente (see photos 1–2, page 14). Allow 6 to 8 minutes. Immediately drain. Pour sauce over cooked ravioli. Sprinkle with Parmesan cheese, if desired. Makes 6 side-dish servings.

***Note:** Freeze remaining ravioli (see tip, page 73). To serve, cook as directed on pages 120–121. Prepare herb-tomato sauce as above; pour over cooked ravioli.

Salmon Stars

Making filled stars is similar to making apple dumplings. They're just smaller.

4 ounces (110g) finely chopped onion
2 ounces (50g) finely chopped celery
1 ounce (25g) grated carrot
1 ounce (25g) butter or margarine
3 ounces (75g) soured cream
1 teaspoon plain flour
8 ounces (225g) tinned salmon, drained, flaked, and skin and bones removed
½ recipe Egg Pasta (see page 68)
½ pint (275g) single cream
1 tablespoon plain flour
¼ teaspoon dried basil, crushed
⅛ teaspoon dried thyme, crushed
1 ounce (25g) grated Swiss cheese

For filling, in a 10-inch (25.5cm) frying pan cook onion, celery, and carrot in hot butter or margarine until tender but not brown. Stir together soured cream and 1 teaspoon flour. Combine vegetable mixture, soured cream mixture, and salmon. Set aside.

On a lightly floured surface roll pasta into a 15x12-inch (38x30cm) rectangle ¹/₁₆ (1.5mm) thick. Cut into 3-inch-wide (7.5cm) strips. Place about 1 tablespoon of the filling on each strip at 2-inch (5cm) intervals (see photo 1, page 88). Cut pasta between mounds of filling, forming 3-inch (7.5cm) squares. Moisten pasta around filling. Form into stars (see tip, below).

Cook stars in boiling salted water until al dente (see photos 1–2, page 14). Allow 8 to 10 minutes. Immediately drain. Keep pasta warm.

Meanwhile, in a medium saucepan combine 2 fluid ounces (55ml) of the cream, 1 tablespoon flour, basil, and thyme. Add remaining cream. Cook and stir until thickened and bubbly. Cook and stir for 1 minute more. Stir in cheese until melted. Pour over cooked stars. Makes 4 main-dish servings.

Making Filled Stars

To make filled stars, cut the rolled pastry into 3-inch-wide (7.5cm) strips. Place the filling at 2-inch (5cm) intervals, leaving a 1-inch (2.5cm) margin around the edges. Then, using a sharp knife or fluted pastry wheel, cut the pasta halfway between the mounds of filling, forming 3-inch (7.5cm) squares. Moisten the edges of the dough by brushing with water. Bring two opposite corners of each square over the filling; pinch. Repeat with the other two corners. Pinch all the cut edges securely to enclose the filling.

Tortellini And Cappelletti

We usually think of dessert as the ending. But the dessert shown here is only the beginning of a collection of tortellini and cappelletti recipes.

The difference between tortellini and cappelletti is simple: One starts with a circle, the other with a square. Pick your preference, then fill, fold, and wrap it around your finger for a delicious twist of pasta.

Nutty Tortellini Dessert

Nutty Tortellini Dessert

A stylish pasta dessert with an outstanding flavour that's reminiscent of crepes suzette. Perfect to serve at your next special occasion.

3	ounces (75g) ground walnuts *or* almonds
1	tablespoon caster sugar
½	ounce (10g) butter *or* margarine, melted
1	or 2 drops vanilla essence
¼	recipe Orange Pasta *or* Lemon Pasta (see page 78)
1	ounce (25g) caster sugar
2	teaspoons cornflour
6	fluid ounces (165ml) orange juice
1	tablespoon amaretto
2	medium oranges, peeled, thinly sliced, and seeded
	Fresh mint sprigs (optional)

For filling, in a small mixing bowl stir together walnuts or almonds, 1 tablespoon sugar, butter or margarine, and vanilla. Set aside.

On a lightly floured surface roll out pasta until ¹⁄₁₆ (1.5mm) inch thick. With a 1½-inch-round (4cm) cutter, cut 48 circles (see photo 1).

Place about *¼ teaspoon* filling in the centre of *each* circle. Fold circle in half and press edges together (see photo 2). Place thumb against fold and bring corners together, pressing to seal (see photo 3). Let stand a few minutes. Cook in boiling water until al dente (see photos 1–2, page 14). Allow 8 to 10 minutes. Immediately drain tortellini.

Meanwhile, for sauce, in a small saucepan stir together 1 ounce (25g) sugar and cornflour. Stir in orange juice. Cook and stir until thickened and bubbly. Cook and stir 2 minutes more. Remove from heat. Stir in amaretto.

To serve, arrange orange slices on 6 individual dessert plates. Place warm tortellini on orange slices. Drizzle sauce over top. If desired, garnish with mint sprigs. Makes 6 dessert servings.

1 For tortellini, use a 1½-inch-round (4cm) cutter to cut the number of dough circles indicated in the recipe. As you cut, gather and cover the dough scraps. Then reroll the scraps as necessary to get the desired number of circles.

2 Fold the filled dough circle in half, forming a half-moon shape. Then press the edges of the dough together with your finger to seal in the filling. It may be necessary to moisten one edge of the dough with water first in order to get the two edges to seal.

3 To shape tortellini, place your thumb against the fold. Then bend the half-moon around your thumb and bring the two outer ends together. Lap one end over the other and pinch firmly to seal. Again, you may need to moisten one end in order to form a seal.

Ham Tortellini With Cheese Sauce

Don't have a 1½-inch-round (4cm) cutter? You can use a 2-inch (5cm) one to cut the tortellini. Just allow a little extra pasta dough to get the same number of circles. You may even find this larger circle easier to shape.

2   **tablespoons finely chopped celery**
2   **tablespoons finely chopped onion**
2   **teaspoons butter *or* margarine**
¼   **pound (110g) minced cooked ham**
1   **beaten egg yolk**
⅓   **recipe Pasta Verde (see page 76)**
1   **ounce (25g) butter *or* margarine**
4   **teaspoons plain flour**
8   **fluid ounces (220ml) milk**
2   **ounces (50g) grated Swiss cheese**
2   **tablespoons snipped parsley**

For filling, cook celery and onion in 2 teaspoons hot butter or margarine until tender. Stir in ham and egg yolk. Set aside.

On a lightly floured surface roll out pasta until ¹⁄₁₆ inch (1.5mm) thick. With a 1½-inch-round (4cm) cutter, cut 96 circles (see photo 1, page 96) and set aside.

Place about ¼ *teaspoon* filling in the centre of *each* circle. Fold circle in half and press edges together (see photo 2, page 96). Place thumb against the fold and bring corners together, pressing to seal (see photo 3, page 97). Let stand for a few minutes. Cook in boiling salted water until al dente (see photos 1–2, page 14). Allow 8 to 10 minutes. Immediately drain.

Meanwhile, for sauce, in a medium saucepan melt 1 ounce (25g) butter or margarine. Stir in flour. Add milk all at once. Cook and stir until thickened and bubbly, then cook and stir 1 minute more. Stir in Swiss cheese and parsley until cheese is melted.

To serve, spoon sauce over hot cooked tortellini. Makes 6 main-dish servings.

Cheesy Tortellini Salad

2   **rashers streaky bacon**
2   **ounces (50g) ricotta cheese**
1   **ounce (25g) grated mozzarella cheese**
2   **tablespoons grated Parmesan cheese**
½   **recipe Whole Wheat Pasta (see page 71) *or* Egg Pasta (see page 68)**
3   **fluid ounces (75g) Italian salad dressing**
4   **ounces (110g) mixed green salad**
2   **ounces (50g) grated carrot**
2   **ounces (50g) thinly sliced and halved cucumber**
2   **tablespoons thinly sliced radish**

For filling, in a small frying pan cook bacon until crisp. Remove and drain on kitchen paper. Finely crumble bacon. Stir together bacon, ricotta, mozzarella, and Parmesan cheese. Set aside.

On a lightly floured surface roll out Whole Wheat Pasta or Egg Pasta until ¹⁄₁₆ inch (1.5mm) thick. With a 1½-inch-round (4cm) cutter, cut 96 circles (see photo 1, page 96).

Place about ¼ *teaspoon* filling in the centre of *each* circle. Fold circle in half and press edges together (see photo 2, page 96). Place thumb against fold and bring corners together, pressing to seal (see photo 3, page 97). Let tortellini stand for a few minutes. Cook *half* of the tortellini* in boiling salted water until al dente (see photos 1–2, page 14). Allow 8 to 10 minutes. Immediately drain.

In a large mixing bowl combine cooked tortellini and salad dressing. Cover and chill several hours or overnight. To serve, add green salad, carrot, cucumber, and radish. Toss gently until well coated. Makes 6 side-dish servings.

*****Note:** Freeze remaining tortellini (see tip, page 73). To serve, cook tortellini as directed on pages 120–121.

Spicy Cappelletti Stew

2 rashers streaky bacon
1½ pounds (700g) beef chuck steak, cut into ¾-inch (2cm) cubes
1¼ pints (720ml) water
1 medium onion, cut into eighths
1 tablespoon instant beef bouillon granules
2 teaspoons chilli powder
1 dried red chilli pepper, seeded and crumbled
1 clove garlic, minced
⅛ teaspoon pepper
1 beaten egg yolk
2 ounces (50g) grated cheddar cheese
1 tablespoon grated Parmesan cheese
⅓ recipe Egg Pasta (see page 68)
4 medium carrots, thinly sliced
3 stalks celery, sliced
8 ounces (225g) tinned sieved tomatoes
1 ounce (25g) plain flour
½ teaspoon caster sugar

For stew, in a casserole cook bacon until crisp. Remove bacon, reserving drippings in casserole. Crumble bacon and set aside. Cook *half* of the beef in reserved drippings until brown. Remove browned beef; repeat with remaining beef. Drain off fat. Return all beef to pan. Stir in water, onions, bouillon granules, chilli powder, chilli pepper, garlic, and pepper. Bring to boiling. Reduce heat. Simmer, covered, 40 to 50 minutes or until meat is tender.

Meanwhile, for filling, combine egg yolk, cheddar cheese, and Parmesan cheese. Set aside.

On a lightly floured surface roll pasta into a 12x9-inch (30x23cm) rectangle ¹⁄₁₆ (1.5mm) thick. Cut into forty-eight 1½-inch (4cm) squares (see photo 1, page 96). Place about ¼ *teaspoon* filling in the centre of *each* square. Fold square into a triangle and press edges together (see tip, below). Place thumb against the fold and bring corners together, pressing to seal (see photo 3, page 97). Let stand for a few minutes.

Add carrots and celery to boiling stew. Return to boiling. Reduce heat. Simmer, covered, 8 to 10 minutes or until carrots are crisp but tender. Add cappelletti and cook until al dente (see photos 1–2, page 14). Allow 8 to 10 minutes more. Stir together sieved tomatoes, flour, and sugar. Stir into stew mixture. Cook and stir until thickened and bubbly. Cook and stir 1 minute more. Stir in bacon. Makes 8 servings.

Making Cappelletti

To make cappelletti, cut the rolled-out dough into 1½-inch (4cm) squares. Fill as directed. Then fold each square in half diagonally over the filling, creating a triangle. Press the edges together with your finger to seal in the filling. You may need to moisten one edge of the dough with water to get the two edges to seal.

Shape the cappelletti by placing your thumb against the fold and bringing the corners together, pressing to seal (see photo 3, page 97).

Pasta Rolls

Give your meal flair with these playful pasta pinwheels.

Making them is similar to making pinwheel cookies or a pinwheel meat roll. But here the tantalising fillings are cleverly rolled up inside long sheets of pasta.

When you slice the rolls, the filling creates a stylish spiral. Serve them at your next dinner party and collect the praise.

Parsley-Pesto Pasta Rolls

Parsley-Pesto Pasta Rolls

½ recipe Oat Pasta (see page 72)
2 bunches parsley, with stems removed
3 ounces (75g) slivered almonds, toasted
1 clove garlic, quartered
¼ teaspoon salt
1 ounce (25g) grated Parmesan cheese
3 fluid ounces (75ml) olive oil *or* cooking oil
Butter *or* margarine, melted

Divide pasta dough in half. On a lightly floured surface roll each half into a 10x6-inch (25.5x15cm) rectangle. Let dry for 10 to 15 minutes.

In a large casserole bring lightly salted water to boiling. Immerse 1 pasta sheet (see photo 1). Return to boiling. Cook until pasta is al dente (see photo 2, page 14). Allow about 3 minutes. Use a slotted spoon to carefully lift pasta and transfer to a colander. Rinse with cold water. Drain well. Carefully spread on a cloth towel. Let stand, uncovered, for 15 to 20 minutes to dry. Repeat with remaining pasta sheet.

Meanwhile, for filling, in a food processor bowl or blender container combine parsley, almonds, garlic, and salt. Cover; process or blend until finely chopped and well combined. Stop the processor or blender several times to scrape the sides. Add cheese. Process or blend until well combined. Add olive oil or cooking oil a little at a time, processing or blending well after each addition; scrape sides as necessary.

Spread *half* of the filling over *each* pasta sheet to within ½ inch (1cm) of edges (see photo 2). Roll up like a Swiss roll, starting from one of the short sides (see photo 3).

Place pasta rolls, seam side down, in a greased 13x9x2-inch (32x23x5cm) baking tin. Brush with melted butter (see photo 4). Bake, covered, in a 375°F (190°C) gas mark 5 oven for 20 to 25 minutes or until heated through. To serve, transfer to a cutting board and cut into ½-inch (1cm) thick slices (see photo 5). If desired, arrange slices on a serving dish lined with spinach leaves. Makes 12 appetiser servings.

1 Bring lightly salted water to boiling in a large saucepan or casserole of at least 8-pint (4.56l) capacity. Then carefully immerse the pasta in the boiling water, as shown. Handle the large pasta sheets gently to avoid tearing them.

2 Spread the filling in a thin, even layer over the pasta. For pasta sheets, leave a margin around the edges as directed in the recipe. For lasagne, spread the filling over the entire sheet.

3 Tightly roll the pasta like a Swiss roll, starting from one of the short sides. Use the towel as necessary to lift the pasta and aid in rolling.

4 Place the pasta roll in a baking tin, seam side down. Brush with melted butter or spoon sauce over the top, as the recipe indicates. This keeps the pasta moist as it bakes.

5 To serve, use a serrated knife to cut the pasta roll into slices. Wipe the knife often to avoid carrying any filling onto the next slice.

Crème de Menthe Pasta Roll

Here's an outstanding dessert that's worth the effort: Chocolate pasta wrapped around a rich and smooth crème de menthe filling.

2 ounces (50g) plain flour
1 ounce (25g) caster sugar
1 tablespoon unsweetened cocoa powder
⅛ teaspoon salt
1 beaten egg yolk
1 tablespoon water
½ teaspoon cooking oil
3 to 4 tablespoons plain flour
1 tablespoon cooking oil
4 ounces (110g) ricotta cheese
3 ounces (75g) cream cheese, softened
1 ounce (25g) caster sugar
1 ounce (25g) plain chocolate, grated
1 tablespoon crème de menthe
   Few drops green food colouring (optional)
3 ounces (75g) plain chocolate, chopped
2 ounces (50g) butter *or* margarine
¼ pint (150ml) evaporated milk
4 ounces (110g) caster sugar
2 tablespoons crème de menthe
8 large strawberries

In a medium bowl stir 2 ounces (50 g) flour, 1 ounce (25g) sugar, cocoa powder, and salt. Make a well in centre (see photo 1, page 76).

In a small mixing bowl combine egg yolk, water, and ½ teaspoon cooking oil. Add to flour mixture and mix well (see photo 2, page 76).

Sprinkle the kneading surface with 3 tablespoons flour. Turn dough out onto floured surface. Knead until dough is smooth and elastic (8 to 10 minutes), adding remaining 1 tablespoon flour if needed (see photo 1, page 68). Cover and let rest 10 minutes (see photo 2, page 68). On a lightly floured surface roll dough into a 12x8-inch (30x20cm) rectangle. Use a sharp knife to cut the dough into four 8x3-inch (20x7.5cm) sheets.

In a saucepan bring water to boiling. Add 1 tablespoon cooking oil. Immerse 2 pasta sheets (see photo 1, page 102). Return to boiling. Cook, stirring gently occasionally, until pasta is al dente (see photo 2, page 14). Allow 4 to 5 minutes. *(Do not boil hard.)* Use a slotted spoon to carefully lift pasta sheets and transfer to a colander. Rinse with cold water. Drain well. Carefully spread on a cloth towel. Let stand, uncovered, for 15 to 20 minutes to dry. Repeat with remaining pasta sheets.

Meanwhile, in a small mixing bowl combine ricotta cheese and cream cheese. Stir in 1 ounce (25g) sugar, grated chocolate, and 1 tablespoon crème de menthe. If desired, stir in food colouring. Spread *one-quarter* of the mixture over *each* pasta sheet to within ¼ inch (½cm) of the edges (see photo 2, page 102). Roll up like a Swiss roll, starting from one of the short sides (see photo 3, page 103). Wrap rolls in clingfilm. Chill for 3 to 4 hours or overnight.

At serving time, for sauce, in a heavy medium saucepan melt chocolate pieces and butter or margarine over low heat, stirring constantly. Stir in milk and 4 ounces (110g) sugar. Cook and stir over medium heat until sugar is dissolved and mixture is slightly thickened and bubbly. Remove from heat. Stir in 2 tablespoons crème de menthe until smooth. Cut each pasta roll into 4 slices (see photo 5, page 103). For each serving, place 2 pasta slices on a plate. Drizzle 1 to 2 tablespoons sauce over and around slices. Garnish with a strawberry. Pass remaining sauce. Store any leftover sauce in the refrigerator for another use. Makes 8 dessert servings.

Greek-Style Lasagne Rolls

½ pound (225g) minced beef *or* lamb
4 ounces (110g) chopped onion
4 fluid ounces (110ml) meatless
    spaghetti sauce
½ teaspoon ground cinnamon
¼ teaspoon salt
⅛ teaspoon ground nutmeg
⅛ teaspoon pepper
⅓ recipe Pasta Verde (see page 76)
    or 8 packaged lasagne strips
1 ounce (25g) butter *or* margarine
1 ounce (25g) plain flour
½ pint (275ml) milk
1 beaten egg
1 ounce (25g) grated Parmesan cheese

In a medium frying pan cook beef or lamb and onion until meat is brown and onion is tender. Drain off fat. Stir in spaghetti sauce, cinnamon, salt, nutmeg, and pepper. Set aside.

If using Pasta Verde, on a lightly floured surface roll dough into a 20x10-inch (51x25.5cm) rectangle. (*Or,* if using a pasta machine, pass dough through until 1/16 to ⅛ inch [1.5 to 3mm] thick.) Cut into eight 10x2½-inch (25.5x6cm) strips (see tip, page 57).

Cook pasta in boiling salted water until al dente (see photos 1–2, page 14). Allow 2 to 3 minutes for Pasta Verde lasagne or 10 to 12 minutes for packaged lasagne. Drain. Rinse with cold water, then drain well. Pat dry with kitchen paper. Spread about *2 tablespoons* of the meat mixture onto *each* pasta sheet (see photo 2, page 102). Roll up like a Swiss roll, starting from one of the short sides (see photo 3, page 103). Place pasta rolls, seam side down, in a greased 12x7½x2-inch (30x19x5cm) baking dish.

In a saucepan melt butter or margarine. Stir in flour and ⅛ teaspoon *salt.* Add milk all at once. Cook and stir until thickened and bubbly. Stir mixture into egg. Stir in *2 tablespoons* of the cheese. Pour over rolls (see photo 4, page 103). Sprinkle with remaining cheese. Bake, covered, in a 350°F (180°C) gas mark 4 oven for 25 to 30 minutes or until heated through. Makes 4 main-dish servings.

Nut-Pesto-Filled Lasagne Rolls

4 ounces (110g) broken walnuts
1 ounce (25g) slivered almonds
1 teaspoon dried basil, crushed
3 tablespoons olive oil *or* cooking oil
8 ounces (225g) ricotta cheese
1 ounce (25g) grated Parmesan cheese
1 tablespoon milk
⅛ teaspoon ground nutmeg
4 heaped tablespoons snipped parsley
⅔ recipe Garlic Pasta (see page 72)
    or 12 packaged lasagne strips
Easy Tomato Sauce

In a food processor bowl or blender container combine walnuts, almonds, and basil. Cover; process or blend until finely chopped. With machine running on high, slowly add olive oil through opening in lid, processing or blending until smooth. Scrape sides as necessary.

In a small mixing bowl beat ricotta cheese until smooth. Add nut mixture, Parmesan cheese, milk, nutmeg, ¼ teaspoon *salt,* and dash *pepper.* Beat until smooth. Stir in parsley. Set aside.

If using Garlic Pasta, on a lightly floured surface roll *half* of the dough into a 15x10-inch (39x25.5cm) rectangle. Cut into six 10x2½-inch (25.5x6cm) strips (see tip, page 57). Repeat with remaining dough.

Cook pasta in boiling salted water until al dente (see photos 1–2, page 14). Allow 2 to 3 minutes for Garlic Pasta lasagne or 10 to 12 minutes for packaged lasagne. Drain. Rinse with cold water. Drain well. Pat dry. Spread about *3 tablespoons* of the nut mixture onto *each* pasta sheet (see photo 2, page 102). Roll up like a Swiss roll (see photo 3, page 103). Place pasta, seam side down, in a 12x7½x2-inch (30x19x5cm) baking dish. Spoon Easy Tomato Sauce over top (see photo 4, page 103). Cover. Bake in a 350°F (180°C) gas mark 4 oven for 25 minutes or until heated through. Makes 6 main-dish servings.

Easy Tomato Sauce: In a saucepan combine 16 ounces (450g) tinned undrained *tomatoes,* cut up; 1 teaspoon *cornflour;* and ½ teaspoon dried *basil,* crushed. Cook and stir until bubbly.

Egg Rolls And Wontons

Think pasta, and Italy immediately comes to mind. But the pleasure of creating pasta traditions isn't solely owned by that Mediterranean country. The Orient has its versions of pasta, too—particularly egg roll skins and wonton wrappers. Tastily filled and fried to crispy perfection, these dishes take your pasta journey to another land.

*Pork and Lobster
Egg Rolls Florentine*

Pork and Lobster Egg Rolls Florentine

Spinach and lobster make a colourful combination in this elegant egg roll filling.

8   Egg Roll Skins (see recipe, right)
1   beaten egg
5½ ounces (170g) tinned lobster, drained, cartilage removed, and finely chopped
4   ounces (110g) finely chopped cooked pork
5   ounces (150g) frozen chopped spinach, thawed and well drained
2   ounces (50g) finely chopped water chestnuts
½   teaspoon garlic salt
    Lard *or* cooking oil for deep-fat frying
    Plum Sauce

Prepare Egg Roll Skins. For filling, in a bowl combine egg, lobster, pork, spinach, water chestnuts, and garlic salt.

Position an egg roll skin with 1 point toward you. Spoon *3 tablespoons* filling diagonally across skin (see photo 2). Fold bottom point over filling, tucking point under (see photo 3). Fold side corners toward centre. Roll up (see photo 4). Moisten point and press to seal. Set aside. Repeat with remaining skins and filling.

In a 5-pint (2.75l) saucepan or deep-fat fryer heat 1½ inches (4cm) lard or oil to 365°F (185°C). Fry egg rolls, 2 or 3 at a time, for 2 to 4 minutes or until golden brown (see photo 5). Carefully remove; drain on a baking tray lined with kitchen paper. Keep egg rolls warm while frying remaining rolls. Serve with Plum Sauce. Makes 8 appetiser or 4 main-dish servings.

Plum Sauce: In a small saucepan combine 4 fluid ounces (110ml) *plum preserves*, 2 tablespoons *white wine vinegar*, 2 tablespoons *soy sauce*, 1 teaspoon *cornflour*, ¼ teaspoon *garlic powder*, and ¼ teaspoon ground *ginger*. Cook and stir until thickened and bubbly. Cook and stir 2 minutes more. Remove from the heat; cool slightly. Cover and chill. Makes 6 fluid ounces (160ml).

Egg Roll Skins

If the dough becomes too elastic during rolling, cover it with a towel and let it rest for a few minutes.

9   to 10 ounces (250 to 275g) plain flour
½   teaspoon salt
4   fluid ounces (110ml) warm water
    Cornflour

In a medium mixing bowl stir together *7 ounces (200g)* flour and salt. Slowly stir in water. Turn dough out onto a lightly floured surface and knead in enough of the remaining flour to make a stiff dough that is smooth and elastic, 10 to 15 minutes (see photo 1, page 68). Cover and let rest for 20 minutes (see photo 2, page 68).

Divide dough into four portions. With remaining dough covered, roll 1 portion into a 12-inch (30cm) square. Sprinkle with cornflour (see photo 1). With a sharp knife or pastry cutter, cut dough into four 6-inch (15cm) squares. Repeat with remaining dough. Set aside the number of skins indicated in recipe. Stack remaining skins in a polythene bag for another use. Store in the refrigerator a few days. Or, place in a freezer container and freeze up to 6 months. Makes 16 egg roll skins.

Wonton Skins: Prepare Egg Roll Skins as above, *except* with a sharp knife or pastry cutter, cut each 12-inch (30cm) dough square into sixteen 3-inch (15cm) dough squares. Makes 64 wonton skins.

1 To prevent egg roll or wonton skins from sticking together during storage, sprinkle the dough with a little cornflour. Place corn-flour in a small sieve and sift over the dough. Shake off any excess before using the skins.

2 Spoon the filling di-agonally across and just below the centre of the egg roll skin.

3 Fold the bottom point of the skin over the filling, as shown. Tuck the point under the filling.

4 For egg rolls, fold the side corners toward the centre of the egg roll. This forms an envelope shape. Then roll the egg roll toward the remaining corner, as shown.

5 Carefully lower two or three egg rolls into the deep hot fat. Fry until golden brown. Frying just a few at a time prevents the oil temperature from falling so low that the rolls be-come greasy. Use a deep-fat frying ther-mometer to monitor the temperature, making sure the thermometer bulb does not touch the bottom of the pan.

Beef-Mushroom Egg Roll

Two of these substantial egg rolls make a main dish.

8 **Egg Roll Skins (see recipe, page 108)**
¾ **pound (350g) minced beef**
1 **clove garlic, minced**
6 **ounces (175g) tinned chopped mushrooms, drained**
3 **sliced spring onions**
2 **ounces (50g) finely chopped celery**
1 **beaten egg**
2 **tablespoons soy sauce**
½ **teaspoon five-spice powder**
   Lard *or* cooking oil for deep-fat frying
   Mustard Sauce

Prepare Egg Roll Skins.

For filling, in a 10-inch (25.5cm) frying pan cook beef and garlic until brown. Drain off fat. Cool slightly. Add mushrooms, spring onions, celery, egg, soy sauce, and five-spice powder.

Position an egg roll skin with 1 point toward you. Spoon about *3 tablespoons* filling diagonally across skin (see photo 2, page 109). Fold bottom point of skin over filling, tucking point under (see photo 3, page 109). Fold side corners toward centre. Roll up (see photo 4, page 109). Moisten point and press firmly to seal. Set aside. Repeat with remaining skins and filling.

In a 5-pint (2.75l) saucepan or deep-fat fryer heat 1½ inches (4cm) lard or oil to 365°F (185°C). Fry egg rolls 2 or 3 at a time, for 2 to 4 minutes or until golden brown (see photo 5, page 109). Carefully remove. Drain on a baking tray lined with kitchen paper. Keep warm in a very slow oven while frying remaining rolls. Serve with Mustard Sauce. Makes 8 appetiser or 4 main-dish servings.

Mustard Sauce: In a small bowl stir together 4 tablespoons *mustard powder,* 2 fluid ounces (55 ml) *boiling water,* 1 teaspoon *horseradish sauce,* and 1 teaspoon *sesame oil* or *cooking oil.* Makes about 3 fluid ounces (75ml) sauce.

Curried Chicken Egg Rolls

8 **Egg Roll Skins (see recipe, page 108)**
1 **whole medium chicken breast (about ¾ pound) (350g), skinned and boned**
4 **ounces (110g) chopped onion**
1 **tablespoon cooking oil**
1 **beaten egg**
3 **ounces (75g) ground peanuts *or* cashews**
1 **ounce (25g) desiccated coconut**
2 **tablespoons finely chopped chutney**
½ **teaspoon curry powder**
   Lard *or* cooking oil for deep-fat frying
   Yogurt Dipping Sauce

Prepare Egg Roll Skins.

For filling, finely chop chicken. In a medium frying pan cook chicken and onion in 1 tablespoon hot oil about 3 minutes or until tender. Cool slightly. In a medium mixing bowl combine egg, peanuts or cashews, coconut, chutney, and curry powder. Stir in chicken mixture.

Position an egg roll skin with 1 point toward you. Spoon about *3 tablespoons* filling diagonally across skin (see photo 2, page 109). Fold bottom point of skin over filling, tucking point under (see photo 3, page 109). Fold side corners toward centre. Roll up (see photo 4, page 109). Moisten point and press firmly to seal. Set aside. Repeat with remaining skins and filling.

In a 5-pint (2.75l) saucepan or deep-fat fryer heat 1½ inches (4cm) lard or oil to 365°F (185°C). Fry egg rolls, 2 or 3 at a time, for 2 to 4 minutes or until golden brown (see photo 5, page 109). Carefully remove. Drain on a baking tray lined with kitchen paper. Keep warm in a very slow oven while frying remaining rolls. Serve with dipping sauce. Makes 8 appetiser or 4 main-dish servings.

Yogurt Dipping Sauce: Combine *4 ounces (110g) natural yogurt,* 2 tablespoons *lemon juice,* ½ teaspoon *onion salt,* ¼ teaspoon *garlic powder,* ¼ teaspoon *turmeric,* and ⅛ teaspoon ground *red pepper.* Makes 4 ounces (110g) dipping sauce.

Chocolate-Filled Wontons

If any of these delectable treats stay around long enough, store them in an airtight container.

32 **Wonton Skins (see recipe, page 108)**
2 **ounces (50g) plain chocolate**
2 **ounces (50g) butter *or* margarine**
3 **ounces (75g) sifted icing sugar**
3 **tablespoon chopped nuts**
2 **tablespoons desiccated coconut**
  **Lard *or* cooking oil for
    deep-fat frying**
  Sifted icing sugar

Prepare Wonton Skins.

For filling, in a small heavy saucepan melt chocolate over low heat, stirring constantly. Cool slightly. In a small mixing bowl beat butter or margarine with an electric mixer on medium speed for 30 seconds. Add 3 ounces (75g) icing sugar and beat until well combined. Beat in cooled chocolate, then stir in nuts and coconut.

Position a wonton skin with 1 point toward you. Spoon about *1 teaspoon* filling just below centre of skin (*see* photo 2, page 109). Fold bottom point of skin over filling, tucking point under (*see* photo 3, page 109). Roll once toward centre. Moisten right-hand corner and lap over left-hand corner; press to seal (*see* tip, below). Set aside. Repeat with remaining skins and filling.

In a 5-pint (2.75l) saucepan or deep-fat fryer heat 1½ inches (4cm) lard or oil to 365°F (185°C). Fry wontons, a few at a time, for 1 to 2 minutes or until golden brown (*see* photo 5, page 109). Carefully remove and drain on kitchen paper. Repeat with remaining wontons. While warm, shake wontons in a bag with sifted icing sugar. Serve warm or cool. Makes 8 dessert servings.

Making Wontons

To make wontons, follow photos 1–3, page 109, using 3-inch (7.5cm) squares of dough. Then roll the skin and filling once toward the centre. Leave about 1 inch (2.5cm) unrolled at the top. Moisten the right-hand corner with water and lap it over the left-hand corner, as shown. Press ends together to seal. Repeat with remaining skins.

Moulded Pasta

Want to turn a few heads? Just wait until you turn this elegant moulded pasta upside down.

Long strands of cooked ziti are coiled around a casserole dish and hold a tasty, cheesy filling. Our detailed instructions ensure success every time.

Best of all, the marvellous flavour of this classy dish will leave your guests' taste buds longing for just one more bite.

Ziti and Cheese Supreme

Ziti and Cheese Supreme

It's important to use the full 8 ounces (225g) of ziti. That way, you'll have the right amount of cut-up ziti in the centre of the mould to help firm up the filling.

8	**ounces (225g) packaged ziti or long macaroni**
1	**tablespoon cooking oil**
1	**ounce (25g) butter *or* margarine, softened**
2	**eggs**
3	**ounces (75g) soft breadcrumbs**
3	**fluid ounces (75ml) milk**
2	**tablespoons chopped onion**
1	**pound (450g) minced raw turkey**
10	**ounces (275g) frozen chopped broccoli**
4	**ounces (110g) Camembert cheese (rind removed), cut up** *
6	**ounces (175g) cottage cheese, drained**
2	**eggs**
4	**ounces (110g) soured cream**
1	**tablespoon plain flour**
	Dash nutmeg
4	**ounces (110g) grated Swiss cheese**

Cook ziti in boiling salted water to which oil has been added until pasta is al dente (see photos 1–2, page 14). Allow about 14 minutes. Drain. Lay ziti straight on kitchen paper (see photo 1).

Spread butter on the bottom and sides of a shallow 3¼-pint (1.75l) casserole. Starting at the bottom outside edge, coil ziti in dish until bottom is covered (see photo 2). Continue coiling ziti up the sides until dish is completely lined. Cover and chill until butter is firm, about 15 minutes. Cut remaining ziti into 1-inch (2.5cm) pieces; set aside.

In a large mixing bowl combine 2 eggs, bread crumbs, milk, onion, ½ teaspoon *salt,* and dash *pepper.* Add turkey. Beat with an electric mixer on low speed to combine. Beat at medium speed 3 minutes. Spread *half* of turkey mixture over ziti in dish (see photo 3). Cover and chill while preparing broccoli mixture.

Cook broccoli according to packet directions; drain. In a bowl beat Camembert and cottage cheese until nearly smooth. Add 2 eggs. Beat until combined. Beat in soured cream, flour, nutmeg, ¼ teaspoon *salt,* and dash *pepper.* Stir in cut-up ziti, broccoli, and Swiss cheese.

Transfer broccoli mixture to pasta-lined dish. Carefully spread remaining turkey mixture over all. Cover *edges* of dish with foil. Place dish in a 13x9x2-inch (32x23x5cm) baking tin. Pour boiling water around dish in tin until 1 inch (2.5cm) deep (see photo 4). Bake in a 350° (180°C) gas mark 4 oven 1½ hours or until firm.

Remove dish from water. Remove foil. Let dish stand 15 minutes. Use a palette knife to loosen pasta from dish, then place serving plate atop dish and invert (see photo 5). To serve, cut into wedges. Makes 8 main-dish servings.

***Note:** If desired, omit Camembert cheese and increase Swiss cheese to 6 ounces (175g).

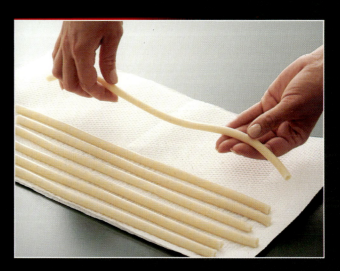

1 Separate the cooked ziti strands and place them on kitchen paper to absorb any excess water. It's helpful to hold the strands upright before you lay them on the paper draining any water that's trapped inside. Make sure the strands lie straight and do not touch. That way, they'll be easy to coil and won't stick together.

2 Begin coiling the ziti strands in the bottom of the casserole dish at the outside edge. Then work in toward the centre. (The ziti strands tend to uncoil if you start in the centre of the dish.) Keep coiling the ziti until the bottom of the dish is completely covered. There shouldn't be any spaces between the ziti strands. The generous butter coating on the inside of the dish acts as a glue, helping hold the ziti in place.

3 Carefully spread *half* of the turkey mixture over the ziti in the bottom and on the sides of the dish. The thick turkey mixture helps bind the ziti, forming a firm wall that holds its shape when you slice it.

4 Pour boiling water around the dish in the tin. The water should be about 1 inch (2.5cm) deep. The water helps distribute the heat evenly through the mould so the edges don't overcook before the centre is done. Be sure to use oven gloves when putting the tin into the oven. The boiling water makes the tin hot.

5 To turn out, run a palette knife around the edge of the dish to loosen the ziti from the sides. Slip the tip of the palette knife far enough down the sides to let air in. Then place a serving plate upside down over the dish. With one hand on the plate and one hand on the dish, invert the plate and dish. Lift off the dish.

Capellini
(fine angel hairs)

Vermicelli
(fine spaghetti)

Spaghetti
(round, thin ribbons)

A Medley Of Pasta

You probably could eat pasta every day for a year and never repeat a variety. Here's a collection of the many choices.

We've listed the common name for each type along with a short description. Use this section to identify a pasta called for in a recipe or simply to expand your pasta vocabulary.

Alphabets
(tiny pasta letters)

Conchiglioni
(jumbo shells)

Lasagne
(broad ribbons about 2½ inches [6 cm] wide)

Acini di pepe
(little peppercorns)

Cavatelli
(curled shells with about 3 ridges)

Tortellini
*(little stuffed twists
or rings)*

Rigatoni
(ridged pasta tubes)

Tripolini
(tiny bows or wing nuts)

Gemelli
(twin twists of spaghetti)

Ruote
(wagon wheels)

Penne (or Quills)
*(smooth pasta tubes
resembling quill pens)*

Ditalini
(tiny thimbles)

Orzo or Rosamarina
(barley-shaped, ricelike pasta)

Fusilli
(twisted spaghetti)

Manicotti
(large, diagonally cut tubes)

Conchiglie
(medium shells)

Conchigliette
(small shells)

Egg noodles
(short, flat ribbons)

Ziti
(long tubular macaroni)

Mafaldine
(flat ribbons about ¾ inch wide)

Cappelletti
(nurse's or bishop's caps)

Spaetzle
(small, irregularly shaped drops of dough)

Anelli
(little rings)

Ravioli
(stuffed pasta squares)

Fettuccine
*(flat ribbons
about ¼ inch wide)*

Ziti tagliati
(cut tubular macaroni)

Linguine
*(oval-shaped ribbons
about ⅛ inch wide)*

Farfalle
(butterflies or bow ties)

Spaghettini
(thin or tiny spaghetti)

Stellini
(little stars)

Macaroni
(short, curved pasta tubes)

Rotelle
(corkscrew or spiral macaroni)

Cooking Pasta

Most cooks cook the way their mothers taught them.

That's probably why there are as many ways to cook pasta as there are mothers in the world. Some cook pasta until it's mushy, others until it's still a little firm. Some add oil to the pot, and others don't.

Keeping all these hints in mind, we chose the best of them and came up with these basic directions and approximate cooking times. Follow them and they'll give you perfectly cooked pasta time after time.

Cooking Directions

5   pints (2.75l) water
1   tablespoon olive oil *or* cooking oil
    (optional)
8   ounces (225g) pasta

In a large saucepan or casserole bring water and 1 teaspoon *salt* to the boil. If desired, add oil to help keep pasta separated. Add pasta a little at a time, so water does not stop boiling. Hold long pasta, such as spaghetti, at one end and dip the other end into the water. As the pasta softens, gently curl it around the pan and into the water (see photo 1, page 14).

Reduce heat slightly and continue boiling, uncovered, until pasta is al dente (tender but still slightly firm) (see photo 2, page 14). Refer to approximate cooking times, opposite. Stir occasionally to prevent sticking. Taste pasta often near end of cooking to test for tenderness.

When pasta is done, immediately drain with a pasta rake or in a colander (see photo 2, page 8). Transfer to a warm serving dish. Serve immediately. To hold pasta for a short time, see tip, page 15. Makes about 1¼ pounds (560g) cooked pasta.

Homemade Pasta (fresh)

Cannelloni	2 to 3 minutes
Cappelletti	10 minutes
Farfalle	2 to 3 minutes
Fettuccine	1½ to 2 minutes
Filled stars	8 to 10 minutes
Lasagne	2 to 3 minutes
Linguine	1½ to 2 minutes
Manicotti	2 to 3 minutes
Mushroom caps	6 to 7 minutes
Noodles	1½ to 2 minutes
Ravioli	6 to 8 minutes
Spaetzle	5 to 10 minutes
Tagliatelle	1½ to 2 minutes
Tortellini	8 to 10 minutes
Tripolini	2 to 3 minutes

Cook frozen or dried homemade pasta a few minutes longer than fresh pasta.

Packaged Pasta

Acini di pepe	5 to 6 minutes
Alphabets	5 to 8 minutes
Anelli	9 to 10 minutes
Capellini	5 to 6 minutes
Cavatelli	12 minutes
Conchiglie	12 to 14 minutes

Packaged Pasta (continued)

Conchigliette	8 to 9 minutes
Conchiglioni	23 to 25 minutes
Ditalini	7 to 9 minutes
Farfalle	10 minutes
Fettuccine	8 to 10 minutes
Fusilli	15 minutes
Gemelli	10 minutes
Lasagne	10 to 12 minutes
Linguine	8 to 10 minutes
Macaroni (elbow)	10 minutes
Mafaldine	10 to 12 minutes
Manicotti	18 minutes
Noodles (medium)	6 to 8 minutes
Orzo or Rosamarina	5 to 8 minutes
Penne	14 minutes
Rigatoni	15 minutes
Rotelle	8 to 10 minutes
Ruote	12 minutes
Spaetzle	10 to 12 minutes
Spaghetti	10 to 12 minutes
Spaghettini	8 to 10 minutes
Stellini	5 to 8 minutes
Tagliatelle	6 to 8 minutes
Tripolini	5 to 6 minutes
Vermicelli	5 to 7 minutes
Ziti	14 to 15 minutes

Nutrition Analysis Chart

Use these analyses to compare nutritional values of different recipes. This information was calculated using a handbook published by the United States Department of Agriculture. Figures are based on the ingredients used in the American version of each recipe.

In compiling the nutrition analyses, we made the following assumptions:
● For all of the main-dish meat recipes, the nutrition analyses were calculated using weights or measures for cooked meat.

● Garnishes and optional ingredients were not included in the nutrition analyses.
● If a marinade was brushed over a food during cooking, the analysis includes all of the marinade.
● When two ingredient options appear in a recipe, calculations were made using the first one.
● For ingredients of variable weight (such as "2½ - to 3-pound [1kg125g to 1kg350g] chicken") or for recipes with a serving range ("makes 4 to 6 servings"), calculations were made using the first figure.

	Per Serving						U.S. Recommended Daily Allowances Per Serving (%)							
	Calories	Protein (g)	Carbohydrate (g)	Fat (g)	Sodium (mg)	Potassium (mg)	Protein	Vitamin A	Vitamin C	Thiamine	Riboflavin	Niacin	Calcium	Iron
Appetisers														
Beef-Mushroom Egg Rolls (p. 110)	228	13	12	13	235	184	20	5	4	9	14	18	2	13
Curried Chicken Egg Rolls (p. 110)	277	12	24	15	217	164	18	2	5	10	10	22	4	8
Parsley-Pesto Pasta Rolls (p. 102)	180	4	12	13	137	141	7	16	22	7	9	4	6	7
Pork and Lobster Egg Rolls Florentine (p. 108)	194	11	23	7	587	203	17	30	10	18	10	10	5	11
Desserts														
Chocolate-Almond-Filled Ravioli with Cherry Sauce (p. 91)	250	5	39	9	35	244	8	18	30	12	12	7	4	8
Chocolate-Filled Wontons (p. 111)	245	2	29	14	137	56	4	5	0	7	4	4	1	4
Crème de Menthe Pasta Roll (p. 104)	360	6	38	21	171	191	9	13	19	5	12	4	11	6
Nutty Tortellini Dessert (p. 96)	218	4	35	7	30	268	7	7	88	17	8	7	4	6
Homemade Pastas														
Apple Pasta (p. 78)	162	5	31	2	100	61	8	2	0	17	11	10	1	8
Beetroot Pasta (p. 78)	160	5	31	2	161	97	8	2	2	16	10	10	2	8
Carrot Pasta (p. 78)	158	5	30	2	162	83	8	99	1	17	10	10	2	8
Corn Pasta (p. 70)	120	4	20	2	149	38	7	3	0	11	8	7	2	6
Egg Pasta (p. 68)	171	6	31	2	149	54	9	3	0	18	12	11	1	8
Egg Roll Skins (p. 108)	50	1	10	0	67	13	2	0	0	6	3	4	0	2
Garlic Pasta (p. 72)	171	6	31	2	149	54	9	3	0	18	12	11	1	8
Herb Pasta (p. 71)	170	6	31	2	149	54	9	3	0	18	12	11	1	8
Lemon Pasta (p. 78)	191	5	38	2	100	60	8	2	9	17	11	10	1	7
Nut Pasta (p. 79)	205	7	27	8	120	132	10	2	0	16	15	10	4	10
Oat Pasta (p. 72)	168	6	29	3	149	78	9	3	0	17	10	8	2	9
Orange Pasta (p. 78)	186	6	36	2	11	172	8	5	50	21	11	11	2	8
Parsley Pasta (p. 73)	171	6	30	2	154	135	9	22	32	18	13	11	4	12

	Per Serving					U.S. Recommended Daily Allowances Per Serving (%)							
	Calories	Protein (g)	Carbohydrate (g)	Fat (g)	Sodium (mg)	Potassium (mg)	Protein	Vitamin A	Vitamin C	Thiamine	Riboflavin	Niacin	Calcium	Iron

Homemade Pastas (continued)														
Pasta Diable (p. 70)	173	6	31	2	161	62	9	13	0	18	12	11	2	9
Pasta Verde (p. 76)	153	6	28	2	113	157	9	39	11	17	11	10	4	10
Tomato-Herb Pasta (p. 79)	179	6	34	2	232	51	9	5	2	20	12	12	1	8
Whole Grain Pasta (p. 71)	141	7	23	3	150	165	10	3	0	17	6	8	2	9
Whole Wheat Pasta (p. 71)	142	6	25	3	150	146	10	3	0	14	5	8	2	8
Wonton Skins (p. 108)	12	0	3	0	17	3	1	0	0	1	1	1	0	1
Main Dishes														
Aubergine Mafaldine Parmigiana (p. 60)	447	19	31	28	1096	431	30	28	19	39	25	26	23	18
Beef and Cheese Manicotti (p. 84)	497	35	33	24	1154	359	54	44	23	23	36	30	27	24
Bolognese Sauce over Pasta (p. 39)	580	30	53	26	434	1117	46	69	81	48	29	48	7	35
Carbonara-Style Penne (p. 33)	478	24	45	22	321	259	36	23	5	41	33	20	27	19
Chicken Ditalini Salad (p. 23)	376	20	19	25	385	605	30	28	52	17	13	32	5	12
Chicken Lasagne (p. 58)	358	26	23	18	463	486	40	93	29	20	28	24	34	15
Chilli-Spaghetti Ring (p. 8)	513	22	67	18	542	402	31	17	11	36	18	32	22	27
Classic Lasagne (p. 56)	373	19	27	21	1046	369	28	38	30	24	24	17	32	11
Crab Manicotti (p. 82)	516	26	32	32	1043	417	40	78	84	23	29	17	31	13
Curried Chicken and Pasta (p. 40)	496	38	54	15	701	513	59	38	47	39	27	81	6	23
Curried Turkey Spaghetti (p. 48)	540	30	59	21	370	614	46	15	5	36	29	44	16	17
Everyday Spaghetti with Meat Sauce (p. 17)	472	18	48	22	1709	201	27	1	0	47	24	23	13	18
Fettuccine Alfredo (p. 14)	405	12	42	21	740	118	19	17	0	34	19	17	18	9
Fiesta Pasta (p. 61)	499	25	32	31	582	358	38	33	60	21	24	29	30	13
Four-Cheese Tagliatelle (p. 32)	516	23	46	26	398	235	35	23	4	35	32	18	45	11
Greek-Style Lasagne Rolls (p. 105)	487	24	45	23	898	440	38	51	16	24	30	23	24	23
Ham and Cheese Stars (p. 92)	494	26	44	24	645	579	40	93	27	39	37	24	26	23
Ham-Pasta Bake (p. 48)	553	27	36	33	741	449	41	45	59	36	33	19	50	16
Ham Tortellini with Cheese Sauce (p. 98)	272	12	23	15	348	237	18	38	13	18	16	10	17	11
Herbed Salmon and Noodles (p. 10)	352	28	31	12	432	975	41	50	8	23	22	42	22	14
Lamb and Feta Layered Casserole (p. 59)	481	28	26	29	824	729	44	44	67	25	24	31	17	22
Linguine with Clam Sauce (p. 32)	516	31	62	13	61	585	48	7	36	55	34	33	14	43
Macaroni and Cheese Special (p. 49)	418	20	36	22	748	363	31	67	15	25	29	13	47	12
Macaroni and Chicken Salad (p. 11)	421	27	35	18	508	456	43	16	9	33	30	41	18	14
Meatless Courgette Lasagne (p. 59)	355	21	30	17	742	281	32	23	21	15	22	8	42	13
Mexicali Bake (p. 11)	699	20	48	47	1121	256	31	22	34	44	29	27	20	17
Nut-Pesto-Filled Lasagne Rolls (p. 105)	483	16	37	31	391	433	25	30	36	25	24	15	20	17
Old-Fashioned Spaghetti with Meatballs (p. 36)	582	32	50	28	1072	661	49	42	61	42	31	50	5	31
Pasta with Four-Cheese and Vegetable Sauce (p. 49)	569	26	47	30	629	556	40	64	16	43	47	27	41	16
Pizza Ravioli (p. 90)	340	14	35	16	1057	149	22	27	25	22	21	17	11	12
Pizza Frying Pan Dinner (p. 10)	484	22	48	23	695	180	33	16	90	28	25	29	19	21
Quick-Fixin' Lasagne (p. 61)	297	23	21	13	640	352	35	34	56	15	19	23	32	11
Ricotta and Ham Cannelloni (p. 85)	492	26	33	28	661	571	40	104	33	30	37	17	40	19

	Per Serving						U.S. Recommended Daily Allowances Per Serving (%)						
	Calories	Protein (g)	Carbohydrate (g)	Fat (g)	Sodium (mg)	Potassium (mg)	Protein	Vitamin A	Vitamin C	Thiamine	Riboflavin	Niacin	Calcium	Iron

Main Dishes (continued)

	Calories	Protein (g)	Carbohydrate (g)	Fat (g)	Sodium (mg)	Potassium (mg)	Protein	Vitamin A	Vitamin C	Thiamine	Riboflavin	Niacin	Calcium	Iron
Rotelle Primavera with Sausage (p. 30)	831	27	43	62	886	665	41	169	97	59	43	30	29	24
Salmon Stars (p. 93)	610	22	39	41	531	452	34	48	7	22	27	34	28	13
Saucy Italian Manicotti (p. 84)	836	23	42	64	1309	1148	35	130	98	59	30	35	17	30
Sauerbraten-Style Swiss Steak (p. 65)	684	35	77	25	1255	571	54	19	8	40	39	44	12	34
Sausage-Spaetzle Vegetable Soup (p. 64)	362	32	30	12	2105	492	50	50	8	19	25	36	19	16
Sherried Veal (p. 44)	897	35	58	57	702	822	53	125	21	51	45	58	21	33
Soured Cream- and Prawn-Sauced Pasta (p. 47)	404	21	43	16	345	545	33	18	14	32	31	31	18	16
Spicy Cappelletti Stew (p. 99)	272	23	20	10	577	382	36	78	13	13	18	21	10	20
Spicy Fish Sauce (p. 38)	382	26	42	11	949	443	41	31	70	35	17	30	4	14
Spinach Pasta Pie (p. 26)	358	13	25	23	406	269	20	59	26	21	22	10	14	13
Taco Pasta Pie (p. 27)	422	24	28	24	603	321	37	27	48	23	21	28	17	20
Turkey Soup (p. 91)	165	16	17	5	727	292	25	38	11	9	10	25	3	9
Ziti and Cheese Supreme (p. 114)	469	37	30	22	637	499	56	38	42	25	36	33	25	18

Side Dishes

	Calories	Protein (g)	Carbohydrate (g)	Fat (g)	Sodium (mg)	Potassium (mg)	Protein	Vitamin A	Vitamin C	Thiamine	Riboflavin	Niacin	Calcium	Iron
Basil Ravioli Salad (p. 88)	345	8	27	23	272	254	12	12	24	20	13	11	5	10
Blue Cheese Fettuccine (p. 47)	230	7	26	11	340	130	11	15	2	15	15	9	9	7
Cheesy Tortellini Salad (p. 98)	228	8	20	14	442	232	12	30	8	12	8	7	10	9
Creamy Macaroni Salad (p. 22)	429	9	20	35	417	105	13	8	2	14	12	7	18	6
Creamy Walnut Pasta (p. 46)	353	10	30	22	345	257	16	19	7	19	20	9	13	9
Fettuccine with Fresh Pesto (p. 52)	285	9	34	13	62	288	14	54	86	28	17	15	15	17
Fresh Tomato-Herb Sauce (p. 39)	148	5	27	2	206	301	7	18	37	21	9	12	3	8
Fruit and Pasta Toss (p. 22)	185	4	34	5	2	223	5	2	36	16	6	6	3	6
Fusilli with Poppy Seed and Almonds (p. 17)	197	6	24	9	566	139	10	4	0	18	13	10	5	7
Grecian Noodles (p. 16)	206	7	24	9	884	115	10	12	10	14	9	8	10	8
Greek-Style Rigatoni Salad (p. 20)	244	6	21	16	300	239	9	19	25	15	7	9	11	9
Herb-Buttered Pasta (p. 16)	195	5	22	10	681	58	7	7	0	17	7	9	5	5
Herb 'n' Garlic Courgette and Pasta (p. 46)	639	4	18	63	852	148	7	52	8	13	9	7	6	4
Italian Rotelle Salad (p. 23)	231	8	13	17	580	175	13	7	10	10	12	9	15	7
Marsala Tomato Sauce (p. 40)	220	7	43	1	750	143	10	21	50	30	12	19	2	10
Mushroom-Filled Ravioli (p. 90)	268	8	20	18	171	224	12	34	9	12	17	9	12	8
Oriental-Style Vegetables and Pasta (p. 33)	123	4	19	3	372	173	6	5	45	15	11	11	1	7
Parsley-Based Pesto (p. 53)	276	8	32	13	53	143	12	20	29	26	14	13	11	10
Rich Mushroom-and-Wine Linguine (p. 41)	213	4	18	12	151	202	6	10	4	13	13	11	4	5
Spaghetti with Whisky-Cream Sauce (p. 38)	446	7	37	23	278	229	11	23	10	27	13	13	7	8
Spinach Ravioli in Herb-Tomato Sauce (p. 92)	160	6	21	6	675	110	9	36	14	12	10	9	7	7
Vegetable Medley in Tomato-Wine Sauce (p. 41)	233	9	42	3	673	437	13	91	140	30	17	19	7	13